Explosive Strength Development for Jumping

by Louie Simmons

Table of Contents

Dedication	3
Caution	5
Introduction	8
1. Maximal Effort Method	12
2. Forms Of Jumping	12
3. Dynamic Method	13

Special Exercises — 18

1. The Importance of Hamstring Training	19
2. Light Hamstring Exercises for Conditioning and Endurance	19
3. Advanced Hamstring Exercises	20
4. Sled Pulling	29
5. Other Methods of Resistance Walking	32
6. Concluding Remarks	36

Strength Development — 115

Developing Dynamic Strength	117
Common Questions Regarding Strength Development Goals	122
Concluding Remarks	123

Medicine Ball Training — 124

Tests	125

General Physical Preparedness — 147

G.P.P.	148
General Endurance	148
Recovery	149

Jumping Volume — 166

Westside Jump Recommendations	167
Box Squat Box Jump	167
Jumping with Ankle Weights	167
Dumbbell Box Jumps	168
Our Sequence	168

Flexibility plus Agility — 234

Concluding Remarks	236
Partner Stretching	260
References	275

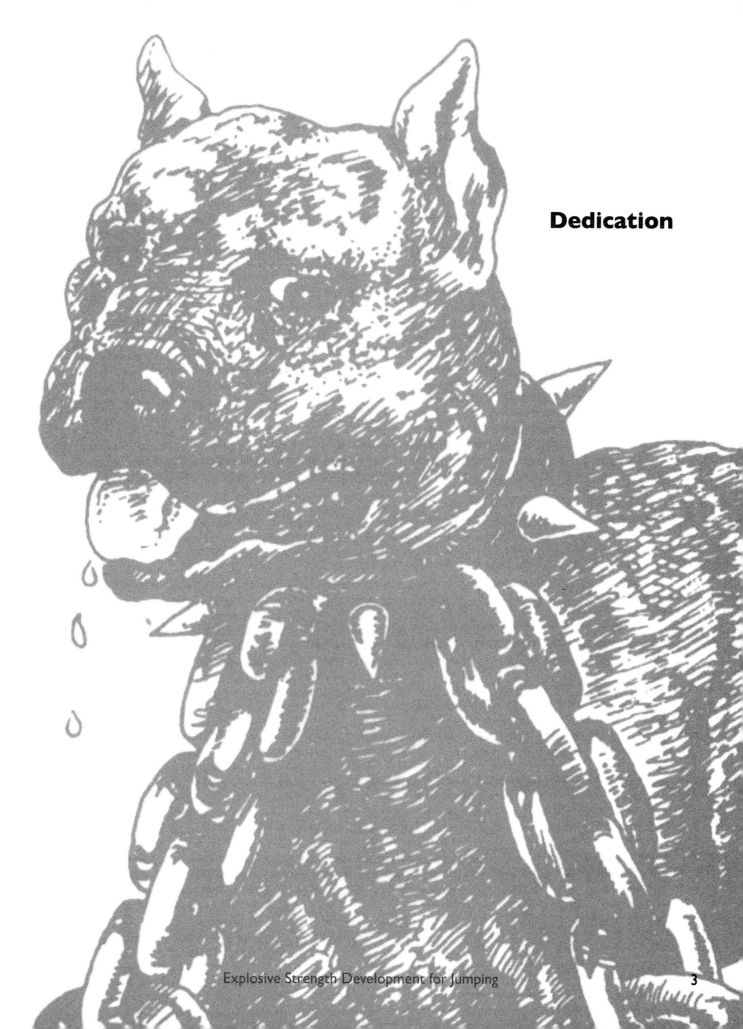

Dedication

I would like to dedicate this book to several distinguished sports scientists who made it possible to write a guide about jumping power. Special thanks are extended to Tadeusz Starzyński and Henryk Sozanski, Ph.D., for their insight and theory on explosive strength training. They laid a foundation for specific forms of jumping ability that not only is utilized in track and field, but all sports involving powerful arms and legs while creating a connection between G.P.P. and S.P.P.

The contributions made by Starzyński and Sozanski to track and field are enormous. Having trained Olympic medalists is the proof their system of drills and programming was successful by combining weight training, bounding, jumping, and depth jumps. The methodologies of these two men were a large part of my ground work for jumping power.

Appreciation is also given to Y.V. Verkhoshansky's endeavors in 1957, focusing on the effect of maximal strength. Verkhoshansky's work on reversal strength were the essence and foundation that led me to my own conclusions regarding jumping higher and farther along with lifting larger weights.

Unfortunately, I never had the honor of meeting these gentlemen who worked diligently on perfecting sports science into a practical system for training. May these small words from one who only wanted to learn more about all facets of strength be heartfelt by my peers.

Louie Simmons

Caution

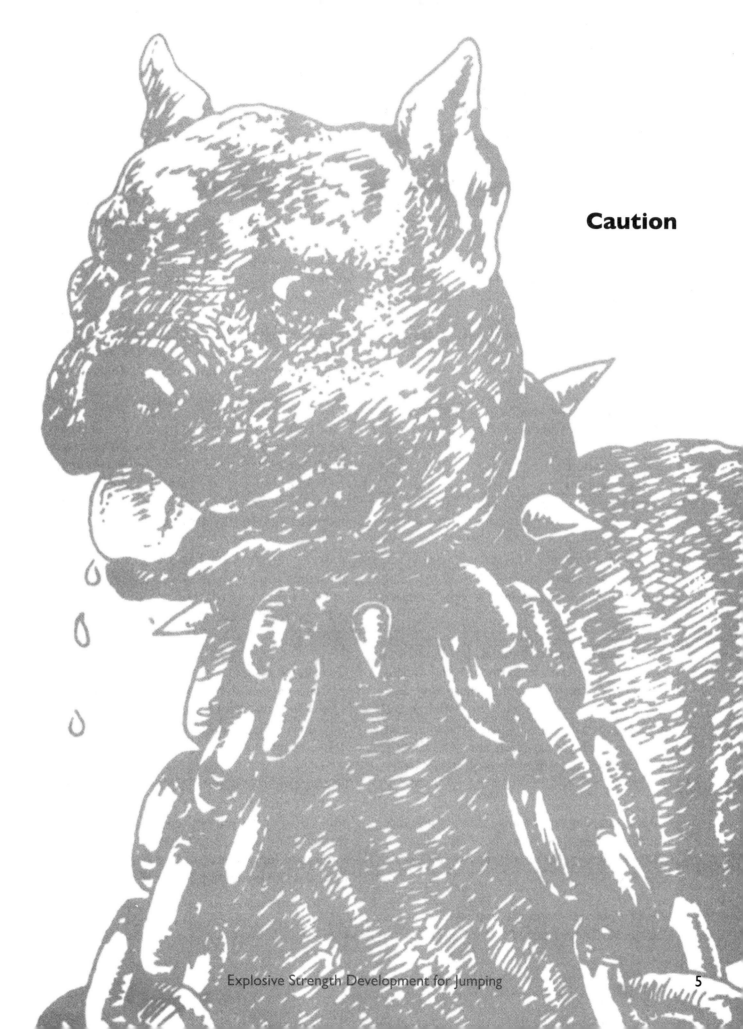

From my observations, far too many sprinters and jumpers are sustaining injuries while training and competing. The main cause of this is Block Style Periodization.

Coaches who train athletes using this style of periodization develop a sound base of General Physical Preparation (GPP) while little or no Specific Physical Preparation (SPP) or tactical work is invested into the athlete.

When the competitive season begins, the athlete loses the given level of GPP in order to sustain the enormous load of high impact training, which is endured while sprinting and jumping. This style of training highly increases the chances of severe injuries.

In addition, many still use the system of breaking training into three specific phases:

Accumulation
Intensification
Transformation

This system is based on the belief of long-term block transformation. This simply means the athlete retains non-specific training, including strength and power training for the complete season.

The Westside System believes once one has mastered technique in sprinting or jumping, most of the training should be increasing GPP. This means endurance specific to sprinting and jumping, especially reducing deceleration during one's approach to the finish line. This System develops Explosive Power through the following techniques:

• Box squatting and sumo deadlifting while including accommodation methods, such as: training that includes bands, chains, or weight releasers.

• Sled power walking in the two styles (*which is recommended and discussed in detail further in this book*): on toes for skill, and on the heels with over-stride for development of the posterior chain.

• Series of jumping on boxes with resistance of all types and depth landing from optimal heights.

Training must and can be blended together throughout the entire year, providing one implements the Westside System and uses a delayed transformation phase for important events.

The Westside System can increase endurance, power, strength, and technique at the same time. It uses special exercises to perfect technique while cutting down sprint times and increasing jumping ability.

This training can and is performed without the epidemic of injuries, unlike Linear or Block Periodization. By continuously repeating the same training, the athlete suffers from accommodation where his or her performance decreases (Zatsiorsky & Kraemer, 1995).

Volume, intensities, and special exercises must constantly be changed: this is *A General Biological Law*. This will avoid adaptation, which is defined as the body's ability to adjust to a specific training regime (Kurz, 2001).

One should always remember that to truly adapt to training is to never fully adapt. Therefore, one must have a transfer of training results, blending SPP and GPP. This can and does co-exist through delayed transmutation.

In conclusion, it is not simply the coach's job to teach one how to jump or run properly. He also has to do his utmost to protect the athlete throughout the yearly plan from injuries, insuring a safe and long athletic career helping athletes fulfill their true sporting potential.

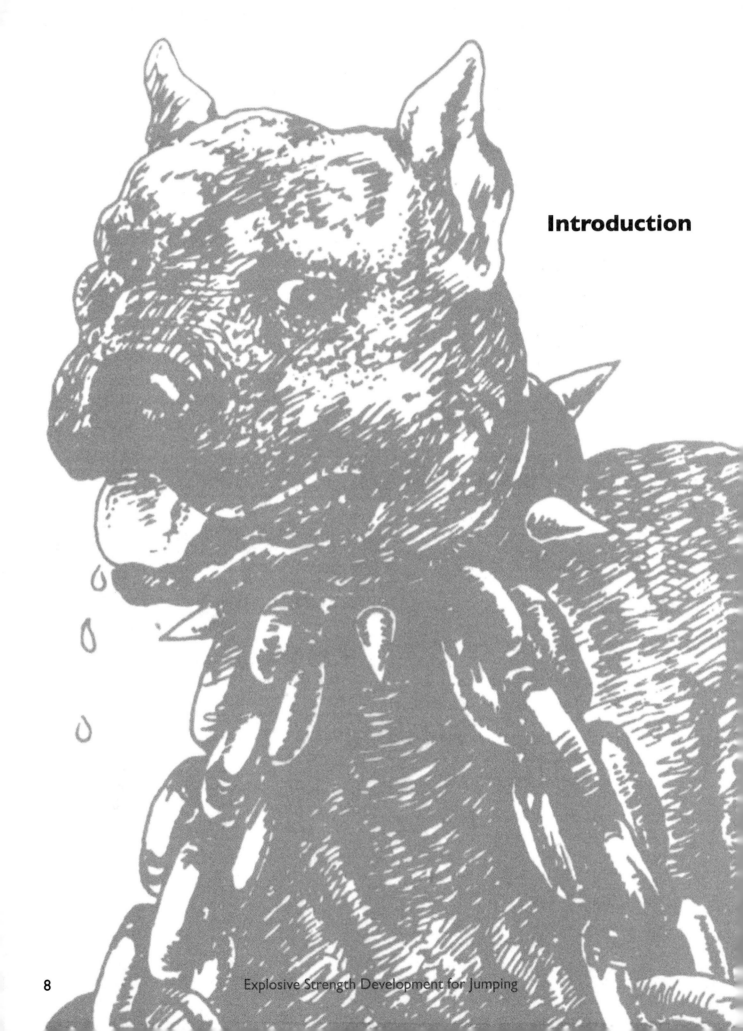

Introduction

I have always been fascinated by how to overcome gravity in order to jump upward or outward while using large weights or one's own body weight. In my quest to find out more on how to overcome such a powerful force, many authors caught my eye with their methods and teachings. Nevertheless, there were a handful of authors who truly inspired and guided me, and these are whom I am going to mention.

Yuri Verkhoshansky proposed using weights above 90% of 1 rep max, (1R.M.), with depth jumps, and of course *General Physical Preparedness* (G.P.P.), in addition to long-term, delayed transformation. Yuri believed that G.P.P. would sustain over a long period of time and would contribute to *Specific Physical Preparedness* (S.P.P.).

Others developed jumping ability with mostly jumping up or down off boxes, in addition to bounding or jumping from the kneeling position with squats, cleans, and snatches.

This system was very successful in producing gold medalists and world records. Tadeusz Starzynski and Henryk Sozanski, Ph.D., developed this system, which is illustrated in their book *Explosive Power and Jumping Ability for All Sports*. Furthermore, Andrezej Lasocki's *The World Atlas Of Exercise for Track and Field* brings the reader a great book for the development of explosive power with light weights, G.P.P. and a series of jumping, bounding, and plyometrics. Overall, their contribution to track and field is amazing.

Today, many throwing coaches believe in just weight training with no throws until the training season turns to competition. Then, they train only throws. I recognized a problem in this. When one approaches his top level of strength and stops weight training in order to focus only on throwing, strength regresses to roughly about 80% of an individual's true strength potential. Therefore, when the total number of throws increases in order to perfect form, the lack of strength can actually hinder perfect form technique.

It is this reduction of strength in vital areas that causes erratic form in an athlete. This is where the Westside System differs as it promotes increasing strength and speed while maintaining or building hypertrophy in the same weekly plan.

To give a better understanding of our system, I will further explain periodization in sports or *Accumulation, Intensification and Transformation* (A.I.T.).

"I have always been fascinated by how to overcome gravity"

Explosive Strength Development for Jumping

Accumulation Phase

Begin with a period of training where athletes use a high volume of G.P.P., concentrating on an intensity of speed that is easy to perform. This period is then switched to the next.

Intensification Phase

The athlete now moves on to S.P.P. work, focusing on a special event or events that one participates in. Rest intervals are longer between working sets. This period is then switched to the next.

Transformation Phase

The athlete now undergoes exercises that help his or her event, using highly specific training methods while eliminating non specific exercises that can interfere with performance.

Westside has condensed A.I.T. periods of training after one has built up a large base of G.P.P. in the early stages of training. Similar to what Verkhoshansky asserts, an individual will use weights over 90% of IR.M. to contrast the training used with jumps, bounding, and Yuri's forte Depth Jumps.

To build maximal strength with weight training, one must add jumping, bounding, and depth jumps to develop explosive strength. This is defined as, *"The ability to rapidly increase force. The steeper the increase of strength in time the greater the explosive strength"* (TIDOW, 1990).

The Westside System has found that most athletes lack some type of special strength, depending on their respective sport. The special strength missing could be a type of endurance such as:

Dynamic Endurance

This is required when repeatedly throwing punches or implements, or when moving the feet repeatedly such as repetitive jumps without a reduction in speed as fatigue sets in.

"One must add jumping, bounding and depth jumps to develop explosive strength"

Isometric Endurance

This is used in such sports as wrestling when a vast amount of isometric holds and actions are being utilized.

General Endurance

This is the ability to complete a given amount of work with competency while maintaining good form. This type of endurance must be raised constantly. Other special strengths that could missing be are:

> *Explosive Strength*
> *Speed Strength*
> *Strength Speed*
> *Eccentric Strength*
> *Concentric Strength*
> *Reversal Strength*

The key to success is knowing what special strength an athlete is lacking, what velocity a particular strength is trained at, and how to develop it. A very good example of this is shown in studies from the former Soviet Union, which writes of junior weight lifters who could out jump junior jumpers for the first three years because of their immense strength.

My background is powerlifting, a sport that clearly demonstrates enormous feats of strength. Therefore, based on my constant research and experience, I have developed a third dimension to be utilized in jump training, which is explained in detail below.

1. Maximal Effort Method

The first is obviously the max effort method. The central nervous system (C.N.S.) adapts only to the demands placed upon it. If there is an inhibition within the C.N.S., it can be reduced by this method of training. This is due to the maximum number of muscle units that are activated with the most optimal discharge frequency.

Basically, this means that nearly every movement in sports such as: running, jumping, lifting, and throwing are a product of maximal strength. A monthly plan of our training system for upper and lower body calls for 24 max-effort lifts above 90% and exceeding 100% in most lifts. These lifts are similar to the actual competition lifts, or lifts mimicking movement in a given sport.

2. Forms Of Jumping

The second is, of course, some form of jumping up onto a box or jumping down off a box, i.e. depth jumps or bounding. Three out of four workouts are done with some form of resistance, such as:

- Jumping while wearing ankle weights
- Jumping while wearing weight vest
- Jumping while holding weights in the hand
- Jumping with a barbell on back
- Jumping with a weighted bag on back
- Combination of 2 or 3 resistances

An example of a basic drop jump onto a high box

Explosive Strength Development for Jumping

A Glimpse Into Westside Barbell

3. Dynamic Method

Russian textbooks state that because of the existence of the explosive strength deficit (F.M.M.), the dynamic method is used not for increasing maximal strength, but to improve the rate of force development and explosive strength. When implementing this method, one utilizes a fast movement against intermediate resistance. For squatting, Westside uses the combination of methods training.

Laura Phelps Sweatt currently the strongest female lifter of All Time

Here a combination of bar weight and band tension is applied. By performing this, one accomplishes two things:

1. Accommodate resistance
2. Provide a faster eccentric phase which in turn produces more kinetic energy

The bar weight is still slightly above explosive strength and slightly less than speed strength. An example of the weight band combination is illustrated in the below table.

(Table 1)-500lb Squat
Based on a 500lb Squat

Percent of 1R.M Used (1 rep max =500%)	Amount of Bar Weight-(Wt), and Band Tension-(Bt) Used	Total Weight Resistance-(Twt) (Wt + Bt = Twt)
50% Of 500lbs	250lb +25% Bt	250 +125=375lbs
55% Of 500lbs	275lb +25% Bt	275+125= 400lbs
60% Of 500lbs	300lb +25% Bt	300+125= 420lbs

The ratio of band tension shrinkage from the top of the movement to the bottom of the movement is illustrated in the below table:

(Table 2)-Band Shrinkage
Band Shrinkage from Top to Bottom of a 500lb Squat

Total Weight Resistance-Twt,(Wt + Bt = Twt) **Top of Squat**	Total Weight Resistance-Twt,(Wt + Bt = Twt) **Bottom of Squat**	Total Amount of Band Shrinkage
375 lbs	315 lbs	60 lbs
400 lbs	340 lbs	60 lbs
425 lbs	365 lbs	60 lbs

This is a new addition to the system because the bands eliminate most bar deceleration. It must be noted that when one raises absolute maximal strength via the max-effort method, the bar speed slows down. However, if one incorporates speed strength, which is between 70-85% of a 1R.M. three days after max-effort training, the sub-maximal weights move at the same speed. To explain this further, I have provided three examples of how the same percent of a 1R.M. should move at the same rate.

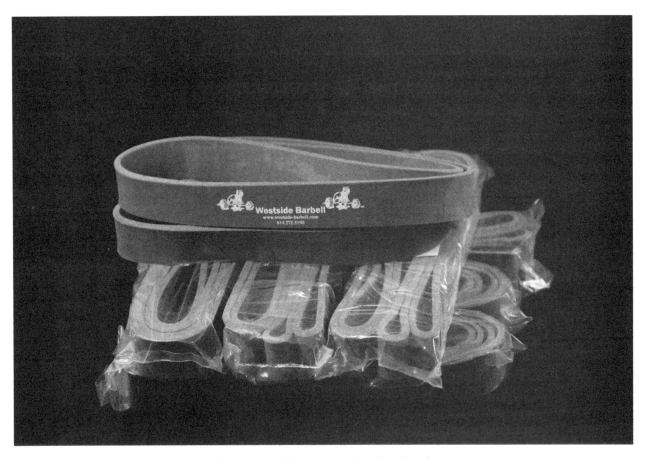

Example of Resistance Bands utilized

1. 300lbs is 60% of 500lbs1R.M squat and its bar speed should maintain .8 to .9 meters per second-(m/s)

2. 420lb is 60% of 700lbs 1R.M squat and its bar speed should maintain .8 to .9(m/s)

3. 540lbs is 60% of 1R.M squat and its bar speed should maintain .8 to .9(m/s)

In simple terms, a 500lb squatter should move his 60% squat weight just as fast as a 1,000lbs squatter can move his 60% squat weight; both roughly at .8 to .9(m/s). By training in this fashion, as one becomes stronger, explosive strength and speed strength also increases. This is explained in full as you read further into the book.

Before moving on to the first chapter, one must realize that jumping is a direct product of explosive strength, and explosive strength is the ability to rapidly increase force. The faster increase in strength in the shortest amount of time contributes to the greater the explosive strength an individual has.

To truly comprehend how to obtain the above strength, one must realize it is the blending of Biomechanics, Physics, and Mathematics.

Biomechanics - Is the ability to learn proper form within all sporting events.

Mathematics - Plays an essential role in controlling the amount of volume for one's strength level. Planning the correct intensity zones ensure the bar speed is correct for the developing of a particular special strength.

Physics - Yes, Physics! It is one of the most important components of strength training. Do you remember Newton's 3 laws of motion?

1. You must learn to overcome inertia by becoming more powerful.

2. Force = Mass x Acceleration, you must understand the relationship between these.

3. Newton's third law comes into play when using the lightened method. Training where bands cradle some amount of weight that is lowered and raised.

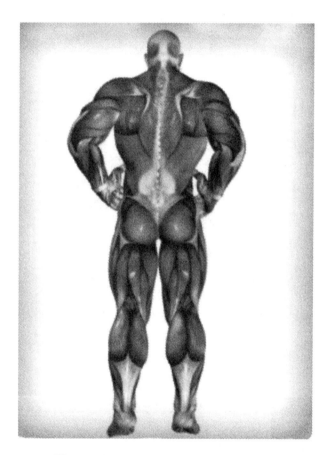

"As you become stronger your explosive strenght and speed strenght will also increase"

How can increasing velocity produce an increase in kinetic energy (K-E), and why is velocity more important in the development of K-E rather than mass?

How is the acceleration of gravity near earth $9.8 m/s^2$ if an individual falls for one second $19.6 m/s^2$ after 2 seconds and $29.4 m/s^2$ after a fall of 3 seconds?

Naturally, a fall of such magnitude would injure a person. However, what would happen if one increased the eccentric phase?

It would increase K-E; this is over-speed eccentrics. Thus, optimal eccentric speed must be learned.

From physics one learns what work is (W=Fd) and what power is (P=W/T). By understanding how to become more powerful, an individual can accomplish work or a sports task, like running a particular distance or jumping a particular height or distance.

Basically, the premise is to explain how to become faster, jump higher, or jump longer. Another example is to contemplate what rule of physics applies when a collision occurs while doing a box squat or a box jump.

As one can see, Physics can be a valuable tool in raising one's sporting excellence.

Let us recap on the formula for developing explosive power for jumping before we go into Chapter 1.

1. Speed strength training with accommodating resistance

2. Maximal effort method - this must be done to activate the most muscle units

3. Special exercises to develop the jumping muscles and eliminate muscular fatigue, including jumps with and without resistance.

Also, remember that to increase a large training base or accumulation phase for novice sled work of all types is used along with special exercises.

My purpose in writing this book is to try and do justice to the long and detailed works of such authors as:

Tadeusz Starzynski
Henryk Sozanski PhD
Andrezej Lasocki
Yuri Verkoshansky- PhD
Tudor Bompa- PhD
Ermakov
Vorobyev
Abadjayev
A,S Prilipin

Their long and dedicated work has led to the development of increasing jumping ability, as well as the programming and organization of planning for optimum athletic performance.

This is just a small list of who has influenced the direction of my training. These men played a huge role in my understanding of special strength and organization of planning the training of all athletes.

Louie Simmons

Chapter One

Special Exercises

Special exercises are used for G.P.P. training that eventually blend into S.P.P. training. This increases one's strength while perfecting form by means of building up lacking muscle groups. Using this conjugate system of training to perfect form helps eliminate the risk of injury to an individual.

Most exercises in this section build more than one muscle group simultaneously, which helps develop co-ordination, balance, and improve muscle recruitment and firing. Special exercises are of the utmost of importance, so pay close attention to the following exercises and guidelines.

1. The Importance of Hamstring Training

The hamstrings play a major role in running and jumping. It is essential that they are flexible and well conditioned for strength displays. Performing the simple exercises below will help prepare the hamstrings to progress into heavier more taxing workouts while reducing the likelihood of an injury. It is worth noting that simple leg curls also serve as pre-hab work. It is well-documented that jumping exercises can be harmful for the knees; therefore, some type of leg curl should be done daily.

A count of 100 to 200 repetitions is a good guideline with 150 reps as optimal. Ankle weights of 2lbs to 20lbs are commonly used.

2. Light Hamstring Exercises for Conditioning and Endurance

The list below provides an example of light hamstring exercises, which are used to develop the required muscles, ligaments, and tendons involved in advanced special exercises including the act of jumping.

It should be noted that beginner athletes must be competent in completing light hamstrings exercises before progressing to more intense exercises.

- Run in place while hitting one's glutes with the heels
- Hold onto a rack jump upward with both legs hitting the glutes with both heels at the same time
- Lie face down, hitting the glute with left leg for reps, then right leg for reps. Lift both legs together or alternate left leg to right leg
- Sit on a bench and hook a rubber band around the ankles to perform leg curls
- Run in place while hitting the heels with the hands
- Pull through with a cable machine or rubber bands
- Perform walking good mornings using a light bar or sand bags on back
- Execute good mornings with a barbell or sand bags while one leg is elevated

All of these exercises can be done slowly or quickly; in addition, ankle weights or rubberbands can be added when possible for more resistance.

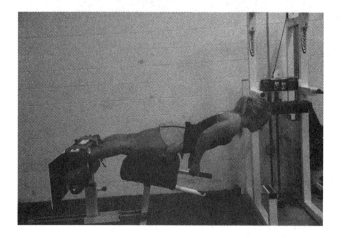

3. Advanced Hamstring Exercises

The below exercises are classified as advanced due to the higher demand placed upon the working muscles and the increase in technical difficulty to perform them:

Glute Ham Raise (G.H.R.)

This was first performed on a pommel horse with a wall ladder to anchor the feet until the calf ham glute bench was invented. The G.H.R. activates the calves and hamstrings at the knee and hip simultaneously. High reps are performed using light weight for conditioning and general endurance. Heavy weight requires low reps of 2 to 6 reps for strength.

Inverse Curl
This exercise used to be preformed while lying on the floor with one individual holding another's feet. They start in the kneeling position while keeping the body vertical. Continue by lowering face first to the floor, and finally returning to the start position. Before Westside Barbell invented the mechanical Inverse curl device that is even superior to the above glute ham raise, this maneuver was very difficult to perform. This patented machine insures that one performs the inverse curl correctly and safely while allowing an individual to go through a full range of movement regardless of body weight and strength ability.

Reverse Hyper
When using this apparatus one can perform a leg curl at the top position, which is very effective for glute ham development while still acting as a traction device.

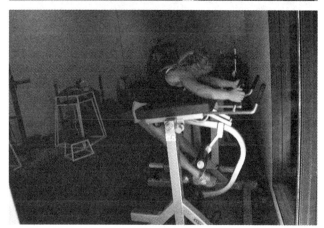

Plyoswing

This originated in the old Soviet Union, and it was a simple swing with a landing surface from which to rebound. Westside Barbell has a plyoswing that incorporates band resistance plus weight resistance; however, barbell weight is the conventional resistance used. In turn, the purpose of band tension is to increase velocity as this is more important than increasing mass.

In regards to programming, it is quite similar to depth jumps. It is important to note that 4x10 jumps work well for the highly trained or the extremely strong individual, and 4x8 jumps can be implemented for the intermediate athlete.

Belt Squat

Westside uses a belt squat machine for squatting, and the movement is performed either on a box or with a regular squat stance. In relation to programming, use heavy weight for strength building with low reps (3 to 5 rep range). Light weights are used for fast reps and sets for predetermined time limits in order to develop a fast rate of force development. An example of this would be the following:

   8 seconds for indoor sprints
   12 seconds for 100meters runner
   25 seconds for 200meters runner
   50 seconds for 400meters runner

The above examples represent the times that are required to run for predetermined distances. For endurance training, it is recommended that one perform 60 reps per minute with rest intervals allowing for recovery. Another variety is to squat while lifting kettlebells in a deadlift or power clean which are very beneficial for the glutes and hamstrings. Consequently, if one rises onto the toes, the calves are forcefully worked.

Belt squat walking for a predetermined period builds the hip, leg, and calf muscles to the ultimate degree. Short duration walks with very heavy weight also build absolute strength. Using lighter weight for long to elongated durations can build great muscular endurance.

Lunges with Kettlebells or Dumbbells

Kettlebells can hang from the sides and sand bags draped across the shoulders could also be used. One can also perform split jumps on the ground or on to boxes.

Explosive Strength Development for Jumping

One Leg Squats

These are sometimes referred to as pistol squats and performed by standing on one leg and squatting while holding onto a rack. This exercise can be executed with bodyweight or some type of resistance such as: barbells, kettlebells, sandbags, a partner, or with a rubberband over the shoulders. They can be done flat footed, heels raised, or rising up onto the toes.

Other Sample Exercises

The illustration below provides special exercises that are highly beneficial for improving jumping ability. *These are presented in no particular order.*

- Jump into a long jump from the knees twisting
- Good mornings with barbell or sand bag
- Good morning with one foot elevated
- Various types of deadlifting such as;

Straight leg	Bent leg	Wide stance	Kettle deadlift standing on two boxes	Kettle deadlift with jumps

- Step ups with barbell
- Jump with barbell off ground from full or half jump
- Regular squat front front or back
- Box squat on to a hard box or foam
- Front squat throwing weights overhead
- Squatting while kicking heels to buttocks
- Walking while holding barbell in front
- Sand bag exercises on thighs
- Walking up or down steps with weight on chest or shoulders

Progression of Exercises

These exercises mentioned above are only a sample of highly beneficial, special lower body exercises. It should be noted that exercises should progress from general movements to develop form and muscle groups to more technical movements implementing such tools as: barbells, dumbbells, and kettlebells.

A detailed and logical progression is provided in the below example, and this order should be adhered to when applied.

```
┌─────────────────────────────────────────────────────────────────┐
│ Sit on the ground and press kettlebells or barbells overhead    │
│ to strenghten all muscles                                       │
└─────────────────────────────────────────────────────────────────┘
                                ⇩
┌─────────────────────────────────────────────────────────────────┐
│ Jump into squat off knees                                       │
└─────────────────────────────────────────────────────────────────┘
                                ⇩
┌─────────────────────────────────────────────────────────────────┐
│ Power clean off knees                                           │
└─────────────────────────────────────────────────────────────────┘
                                ⇩
┌─────────────────────────────────────────────────────────────────┐
│ Power snatch off knees                                          │
└─────────────────────────────────────────────────────────────────┘
                                ⇩
┌─────────────────────────────────────────────────────────────────┐
│ Split snatch off knees                                          │
└─────────────────────────────────────────────────────────────────┘
                                ⇩
┌─────────────────────────────────────────────────────────────────┐
│ Power clean off knees while jumping onto the feet               │
└─────────────────────────────────────────────────────────────────┘
                                ⇩
┌─────────────────────────────────────────────────────────────────┐
│ Power snatch off knees onto feet                                │
└─────────────────────────────────────────────────────────────────┘
                                ⇩
┌─────────────────────────────────────────────────────────────────┐
│ Power split snatch off knees onto feet                          │
└─────────────────────────────────────────────────────────────────┘
```

4. Sled Pulling

General conditioning is the concurrent building of cardiovascular efficiency and muscular development. One piece of equipment that significantly increases both is the Sled, which is an effective yet highly underestimated strength and conditioning tool. To perform this technique, one should begin by power walking with long strides, pulling with the heels. This works as a glute-hamstring extension while also building the calves and hips (*both front and back*). Remember always walk and never run with a sled.

How to Operate

To generate optimal power for each step, one must pull violently when the heel touches the ground. The movement is similar to walking in a non-motorized treadmill. The optimal distance to pull a sled is for 60 yards a trip. This works for all styles of jumping (upward, outward, or sideways), and for short sprints. Rest intervals between trips depend on an individual's level of physical preparedness. Moreover, long distance sled pulling builds G.P.P. and greater endurance of all types.

Sled Programming

Monday: The heaviest weight pulls should be completed. The smallest numbers of 60yard trips are performed powerfully eight times. Remember the last step must be as dominant as the first in order to eliminate deceleration. The primary objective of this training day is absolute strength development.

Wednesday: Lower the weight on the sled and add trips; average 12 trips with a reduction of 30% of weight on the sled. Building strength endurance is the purpose of this training day.

Friday: Weight is again reduced by 30% of the heaviest weight used on Monday's workout. The goal of this training day serves two needs:

1. A warm up for Friday's dynamic squats or deadlifts

2. Restoration work from previous training day

The weights used for sled dragging can range from 25lbs for children up to 300lbs for an elite athlete as an NFL lineman. If an individual staggers from side to side while dragging the sled, this is an indication that there is too much weight on the sled.

Sled Variations and Considerations
The power sled work can be varied to develop different muscle groups by simply doing the following:

- Going forward on the balls of the feet

- Stepping sideward with long explosive steps

- Walking backwards

- Using ankle weights

- Pushing a weighted wheel barrow while dragging a sled (*Max effort exercise*)

- Up and down hill dragging

Bent over sled drags target, develop and condition the hamstrings. To learn more about this and other exercises purchase our G.P.P DVD from www.westside-barbell.com

Another way to vary sled dragging is to use a weighted vest, which is usually around 10lbs for children and up to 75lbs for an N.F.L. lineman. This adds strength to the legs, hips, and abs. If one cannot afford a weighted vest, a simple and inexpensive version could be a hooded, long-sleeve sweatshirt that has been soaked in water.

Finally, it is worth noting that the correct weight on a sled can perfect the proper form or lean that an individual needs for optimal technique. Basically, it teaches an individual how to utilize gravity to assist his running rather than hinder it. Remember to power walk and not run.

Wheelbarrow walking is a total body exercise. It will build a tremendously strong torso while simultaneously building and conditioning the posterior chain. To learn more about this and other exercises purchase our G.P.P DVD from www.westside-barbell.com

Explosive Strength Development for Jumping

5. Other Methods of Resistance Walking

Non-Motorized Treadmill

When using a non motorized treadmill, weight vests and ankle weights can be added. Furthermore, rubber bands can be attached around the shoulders, waist, upper thigh, or ankles. This style of workout can be very taxing due to the increase of steps per minute. Remember one can walk forward, backward, or sideways on this machine. It is worth noting that sideways walking along with correct form in squatting and deadlifting can almost eliminate the necessity to perform lateral drills, thus saving time.

Belt Squat

This belt squat serves an unparalleled resistance walking device as it can immensely develop the legs, hips, and glutes. It is performed when one walks forwards or backwards or waddles from side to side with the feet spread slightly wider than shoulder width.

Ankle Weights and Weighted Vests

These can be used independently of each other or simultaneously for a predetermined distance; they can also be implemented for duration.

Large Exercise for Jumping

What part does squatting, deadlifting, and good mornings play in the training of jumpers and sprinters? Answer= A LARGE AMOUNT

To raise absolute strength, the maximum effort method takes precedence. Yuri Verkhoshansky used a contrast system of using 90% to 95% squats in the first part of the workout; then, speed strength squats followed, ranging 75% to 85% to cause a slow-fast contrast.

Westside employs the maximum effort method in maximum intensity, meaning an all-time record in a variation of a squat, deadlift, or good morning. Max effort day should be on Monday just after competing and 72 hours between dynamic days.

"Focus should be placed on the weakest muscle group"

Max Effort Day

The maximal effort method is superior for improving both intramuscular and intermuscular coordination as it simply recruits the most muscles.

Working up to an all-time record maximum as fast as possible can minimize training volume. Westside research has shown that one weight should be taken at 90%, a second close to an individual's current record, and the 3rd at a small personal record. Then, progress to two or three special exercises for the posterior chain, which includes the lower back.

Focus should be placed on the weakest muscle group when selecting special exercises. Science has proven that when using exercises at 90% and above for three weeks, a person's C.N.S. tends to regress.

However, Westside has overcome this by switching major bar exercises each week. An example would be switching exercises from a squat, deadlift, or good morning variation. The order selected does not matter as long as it is done once per week.

Maximum strength is the measure in time to complete the lift, not the amount of weight on the bar. All max effort lifts complement each other. This means each variation of a max lift helps build another; this, in turn, aids in developing more explosive power.

Josh Connely deadlifting 800lbs

Max Effort Lifts

TYPE OF MOVEMENT	NAME OF LIFT
Squat	Box Squat
Squat	Front Squat
Squat	Back Squat
Squat	14 Inch Cambered Bar
Squat	Bow Bar
Squat	Zercher Squat
Squat	Belt Squat On A Hard Box
Squat	Belt Squat On A Soft Box
Squat	Belt Squat With No Box
Squat	Squat With Chains
Squat	Squat With Bands
Squat	Squat With Weight Releasers

TYPE OF MOVEMENT	NAME OF LIFT
Good morning	Arch Back
Good morning	Rounded Back(Not Lower Back)
Good morning	Wide Stance
Good morning	Close Stance
Good morning	Front Foot Elevated
Good morning	Squat Bar
Good morning	14inch Cambered Bar
Good morning	Sand Bag On Back
Good morning	Band Good Morning

TYPE OF MOVEMENT	NAME OF LIFT
Pulling	Snatch Grip (Wide)
Pulling	Snatch Grip (Closer)
Pulling	Power Clean
Pulling	Snatch Grip (Wide) Standing On A 2 Inch Box
Pulling	Snatch Grip (Closer) Standing On A 2 Inch Box
Pulling	Power Clean Standing On A 2 Inch Box
Pulling	Snatch Grip (Wide) Plates Elevated On A 2 Inch Box
Pulling	Snatch Grip (Closer) Plates Elevated On A 2 Inch Box
Pulling	Power Clean Plates Elevated On A 2 Inch Box
Pulling	Standing On A 2 Or 4 Inch Box
Pulling	Kettlebell Clean

Dynamic Effort Day

This method increases and improves the rate of force development and explosive strength, which is discussed in depth within the Science and Practice of Strength Training (V.M. Zatsiorsky, 1995).

The dynamic effort method is performed in a three week wave for 50% to ^0% of a 1R.M.

For sports of all types Westside suggests the following:

Week 1 12 Sets of 2 Reps
Week 2 12 Sets of 2 Reps
Week 3 10 Sets of 2 Reps

This system is designed to control volume at a predetermined intensity of a 1 R.M. When maintained, the bar speed should be roughly .8m/s. This is a very vital factor for success. The average rest interval between sets is 60 seconds to as short as one's level of preparedness allows.

All workouts must be finished within 45 minutes in order to maintain high levels of testosterone.

For greater details on organizing and programming, one should see the *Book Of Methods* by Louie Simmons.

The most common lifts for dynamic waves is as follows:

Powercleans
Powersnatch
Squat
Bench
Deadlift

Consequently, through reading the articles by Louie Simmons, one should develop a good understanding of the waves for max effort day, which encompass three week waves for explosive and speed strength while changing each week.

Provided below is a list of exercises to use for explosive and speed strength. Always use the combination method for explosive and speed strength wave to eliminate bar deceleration .This teaches acceleration strength throughout the entire range of motion.

6. Concluding Remarks

Barbell squats and deadlifts are preferred to increase jumping and sprinting as they greatly improve absolute, explosive, and speed strength. As these strengths increase, they will clearly aid the ability to overcome one's body weight. Therefore, the sets must be high and reps low to increase strength while limiting muscle mass. In regards to exercise selection, it is as simple as using the imagination. However, when selecting exercises, it is vital that close attention is paid to the event; carefully select the special strengths relevant to a specific sport and develop the muscle groups that need the most attention.

When selecting, try to avoid mechanical standing and lying hamstring machines as they are a highly ineffective exercise resistance tool. The actions of these devices start at the knees, then move onto the glutes. This can be very dangerous, unlike the mechanical examples given in this chapter.

Many people ask the question about how to change the programming for age and gender. The Westside System can and has been used with any age or gender because the system is based on math for correct loading; thus, making it possible for a novice or advanced individual to train optimally for his strength level and fitness level.

The Westside System bridges the gaps between G.P.P. and S.P.P. for the goal of increasing strength in the body, which plays a major role in improving a particular motion relative to one's sport.

Barbell front squat

Balgarian split squat

Ankle weight leg curls

Explosive Strength Development for Jumping

Kettlebell swing

Banded kettlebell swing

Banded glute-ham raise

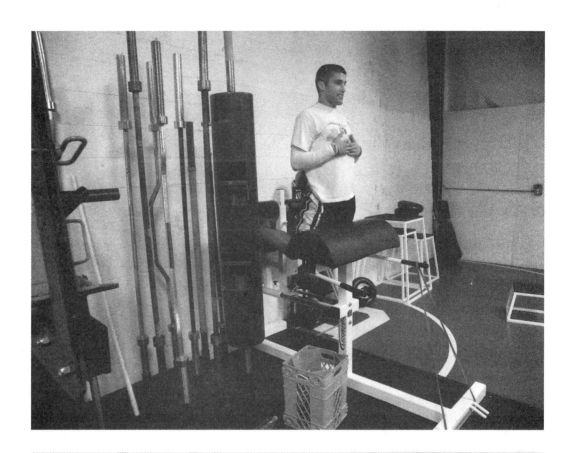

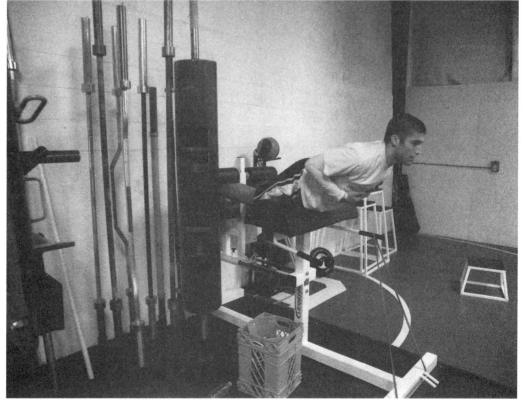

Glute-ham raise

Med ball glute-ham raise

Knees-to-feet jump with barbell on back

Explosive Strength Development for Jumping

Barbell step-up

Box jump with weighted vest

Single leg barbell high pull

Back extension with giant cambered bar

Explosive Strength Development for Jumping

Knees-to-feet jump with barbell overhead finish

Split squat or walking lunge with snatch grip overhead barbell

Split squat or walking lunge with barbell

Split squat or walking lunge with front squat barbell rack

Explosive Strength Development for Jumping

Dumbbell walking lunge

Kettlebell walking lunge

Overhead kettlebell walking lunge

Kettlebell step-up with opposing knee drive

Dumbbell step-up with opposing knee drive

Explosive Strength Development for Jumping

Bodyweight single leg box squat

Barbell single leg box squat

Kettlebell deep squat

Belt-squat box squat

Barbell lateral lunge

Bodyweight jumping split squats

Explosive Strength Development for Jumping

Single leg box squat box jump

Banded belt-to-feet box squat

Banded cross body power rack free squat

Banded good morning

Banded pull-through

Banded pull-through with banded good morning

Explosive Strength Development for Jumping 65

Dumbbell glute-ham raise

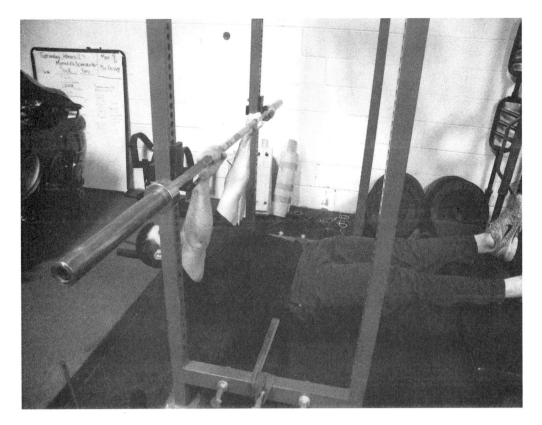
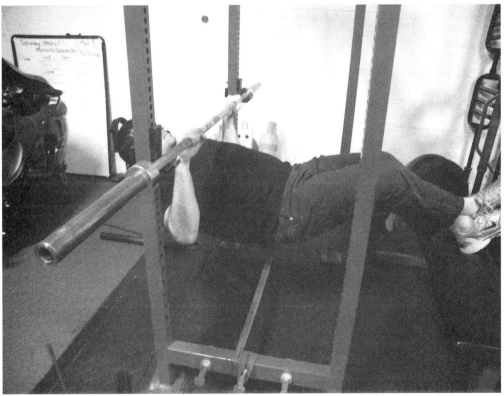

Band resisted bench pull-up

Explosive Strength Development for Jumping

Single leg physio ball leg curl

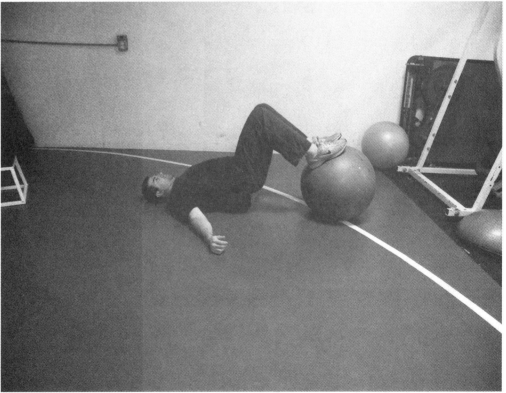

Double leg physio ball leg curl

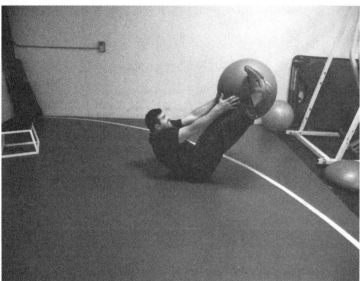
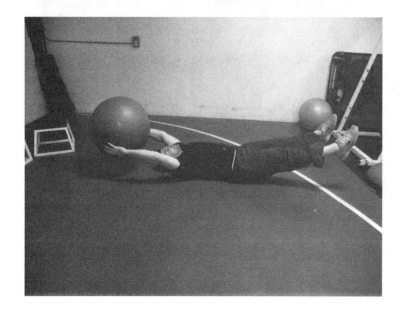

Straight leg physio ball transfer

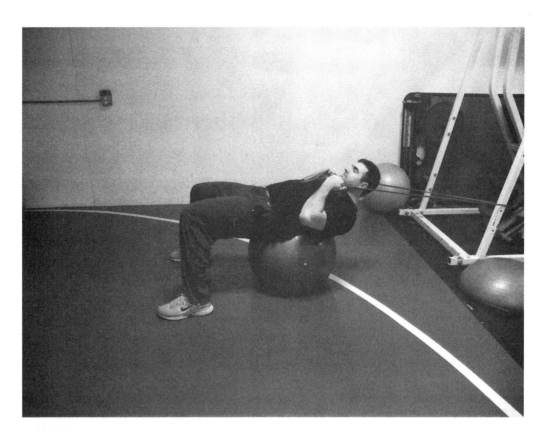

Physio ball crunch

Standing weighted crunch

Hanging straight leg raise

Hanging dumbbell knee drive

Dumbbell side bend

Explosive Strength Development for Jumping

Lying dumbbell straight leg raise

1 arm elbow-in dumbbell row

1 arm elbow-out dumbbell row

2 arm dumbbell upright row

2 arm dumbbell hang clean

Sinegle arm dumbbell snatch

2 arm kettlebell triceps extension

Single arm kettlebell hang clean

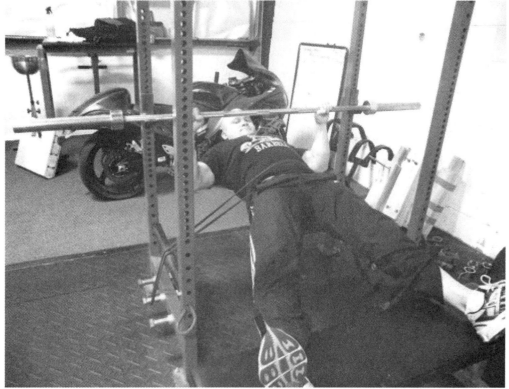

Wide feet band resisted bench pull-up

Wide grip laterals pull-down

2 arm chain triceps extension

2 arm chain bench press

2 arm chain incline press

2 arm chain incline triceps extension

2 arm chain decline press

2 arm chain decline triceps extension

Decline bench knee drive

Decline bench straight leg raise

Wide grip pull-up with weighted vest

Explosive Strength Development for Jumping

Band tare with palms down

Pike pull-up

Band resisted wide grip pull-up

2 arm dumbbell Williams's extension

2 arm dumbbell roll-back's

Hanging bar toe touch

Decline straight-arm med ball twist

Decline med ball throw back

EZ bar triceps extension

Bodyweight box jump

Prowler push

Safety bar seated good mornings

Bamboo bar bench press

Safety bar back extension

Cross arm front squat

Barbell step-ups with chain resistance

Partner mirrored overhead press

Explosive Strength Development for Jumping 107

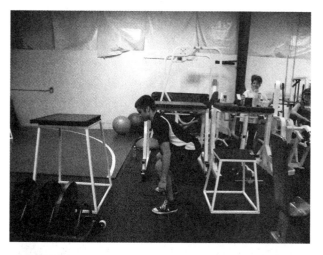

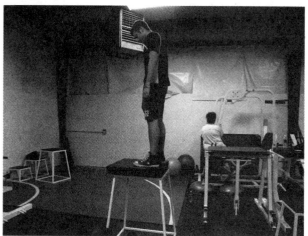

Depth jump

Reverse sled pull

Sled pull

Explosive Strength Development for Jumping

Single-leg box jump with ankle weights

Safety bar step-ups with chain resistance

Explosive Strength Development for Jumping

Knee-to-feet box jump

Band resisted foam roll crunch

45° barbell row

Chapter Two

Strength Development

As an individual becomes stronger, he does not need to worry about gaining weight. Body weight should actually be kept to a minimum because the heavier an individual, the more gravitational pull he must overcome.

It may be argued that a larger more powerful runner may produce more force due to size and strength. However, such an athlete would be at a disadvantage in comparison to a lighter runner who generates more force relative to his bodyweight. This is due to the lighter runner having a more powerful relationship to his body mass. Therefore, it is essential to produce stronger muscles in order to increase force while eliminating high rep exercises to avoid excessive muscle hypertrophy. Barry Ross certainly realized this fact within his book Underground Secrets to Faster Running. Ross quotes a study in running biomechanics that illustrated that 90% of running force is used vertically and only 10% horizontally, which further clarifies that one must get as strong as possible while holding bodyweight at a minimum in order to become a more efficient runner. Similarly, Berger, an American researcher, found that different training programs at different percentages gave much different results in a specific training strength that added muscle mass.

While other programs of a certain rep and set scheme had other results such as no added muscle mass. In my opinion, this is a mistake because all weights whether heavy or light, lifted slowly or lifted quickly, should be trained inside of a weekly plan. If this fundamental principle is not adhered to, detraining of a specific special strength can occur. Therefore, selecting a correct method of training is essential for developing optimal strength.

"It is essential to produce stronger muscles in order to increase force"

Developing Dynamic Strength

The Westside training system, also referred to as combination resistance training, is the correct, safest and most efficient training method that one could chose for strength development.

A core component of this training method for athletic development is its three week wave to develop dynamic strength.

The optimal percentage to implement for the training cycle was obtained thanks to the research of A.S. Prilipins, who discovered that explosive-strength is developed at 30% to 40% of a 1 rep max and speed-strength is developed at 75% to 85% of a 1 rep max. The Westside System trains in the middle of these two strengths. This utilizes weights ranging from 50% to 60% of a 1.Rm with accommodating resistance for sets of two reps.

Consequently, the system trains at a higher intensity zone than explosive strength and at slightly lower intensity zone than speed strength. Below is a table illustrating this point further.

Table 3

Percent of Bar weight based off a 1R.M squat	Percent of Band tension provide at the Top of the squat	Total Bar Weight= Barbell weight +band tension
50%	25%	75%
55%	25%	80%
60%	25%	85%
Percent of Bar weight based off a 1R.M squat	Percent of Band tension provide at the Bottom of the squat	Total Bar Weight= Barbell weight +band tension
50%	10%	60%
55%	10%	65%
60%	10%	70%

While the above percentages are for explosive strength, the band tension can eliminate most bar deceleration thus prolonging force development. Refer to the *Squat and Deadlift* Manual for in-depth instruction regarding technique, bar speed and recovery.

The Westside system is mathematical, meaning it works for athletes of any strength, gender or age. The following tables illustrate this concept.

Table 4
This 3 week wave is based on an individual who has a 200lb max squat.

	Percent Of Bar Weight Based Off A 1R.M Squat	Total Band Tension	Reps	Sets	Total Lifts
Week 1	50%=100lb	50lbs	2	12	24
Week 2	55%=110lb	50lbs	2	12	24
Week 3	60%=120lb	50lbs	2	10	20
Total Volume = 2400lbs Bar Speed = .8/ms					

Table 5
This 3 week wave is based on an individual who has a 300lb max squat.

	Percent Of Bar Weight Based Off A 1R.M Squat	Total Band Tension	Reps	Sets	Total Lifts
Week 1	50%=150lb	50lbs	2	12	24
Week 2	55%=165lb	50lbs	2	12	24
Week 3	60%=180lb	50lbs	2	10	20
Total Volume=3600lbs Bar Speed = .8/ms					

Table 6
This 3 week wave is based on an individual who has a 400lb max squat.

	Percent Of Bar Weight Based Off A 1R.M Squat	Total Band Tension	Reps	Sets	Total Lifts
Week 1	50%=200lb	100lbs	2	12	24
Week 2	55%=220lb	100lbs	2	12	24
Week 3	60%=240lb	100lbs	2	10	20
Total Volume=4800lbs Bar Speed = .8/ms					

Table 7
This 3 week wave is based on an individual who has a 500lb max squat.

	Percent Of Bar Weight Based Off A 1R.M Squat	Total Band Tension	Reps	Sets	Total Lifts
Week 1	50%=250lb	125lbs	2	12	24
Week 2	55%=275lb	125lbs	2	12	24
Week 3	60%=300lb	125lbs	2	10	20
Total Volume=6000lbs Bar Speed = .8/ms					

As one can see the percents, total lifts and bar speed are the same for each individual regardless of his total max squat.

Hopefully, this emphasizes how the Westside system of training can be implemented for any individual by using the correct mathematics that correlates to his given strength level.

It should be noted that it is essential for one to have a different 1R.M with diverse squat variations and bars in order to provide a different training stimulus. Variances can include the following:

- 14" chambered bar Squat
- Max
- Front Squat Max
- Overhead Squat Max
- Zercher Squat Max
- Safety Squat Max
- Manta Ray Squat Max

Think Outside the box when creating a max effort exercises

By having an array of squat maxes, it allows one to have a selection of lifts to base the individual three week wave upon.

To illustrate this further, Table 8 depicts a 9 week preparatory phase cycle, leading into the track season for an athlete who has a squat of 700lbs with a safety squat bar.

Table 8

	Percent Of Bar Weight Based Off A 1R.M Squat	Total Band Tension	Reps	Sets	Total Lifts
Week 1	50%=325lb	70lbs=Light	2	8	16
Week 2	55%=375lb	70lbs=Light	2	8	16
Week 3	60%=415lb	70lbs=Light	2	6	12
For The Next Wave Changing Band Tension As A New Training Stimulus					
Week 4	50%=325lb	140lbs=Medium	2	8	16
Week 5	55%=375lb	140lbs=Medium	2	8	16
Week 6	60%=415lb	140lbs=Medium	2	6	12
For The Next Wave Changing Band Tension As A New Training Stimulus					
Week 7	50%=325lb	250lbs=Strong	2	8	16
Week 8	55%=375lb	250lbs=Strong	2	8	16
Week 9	60%=415lb	250lbs=Strong	2	6	12

In the above sample, it is clearly that the band tension was changed in order to provide a new training stimulus after each individual three week cycle. However, one can also change to a different bar for a three week cycle, providing he has a 1R.M on the given bar being in order to base calculations upon. The same bar should be used for each individual three week wave and always implement chains, bands or both to reduce bar deceleration.

Explosive Strength Development for Jumping

Common Questions Regarding Strength Development Goals

How to incorporate dynamic work to enhance power cleans and snatches?

When performing power cleans and power snatches, use a three week wave with 70%, 75% and 80% of one's 1 R.M., remembering to keep the weight lifted at 70% range to its optimal amount (18 lifts) and when training at 80% range keep the weight lifted to its optimal amount (15 lifts).

How to incorporate the combination method to improve sumo deadlifts?

When using the combination method to perform sumo deadlifts, keep the bar weight at 50% of a 1R.M. Note that 30% band tension will be at the top of the lift, and 10% band tension will be at the bottom of the lift. This yields 60% at the bottom and 80% at the lock out.

Can weight releasers be utilized for dynamic work?

When using weight releasers, the combined weight of the barbell plus weight releaser should have a combined poundage of 80% of one's 1R.M. Therefore, load 20% of the amount on the weight releasers and 60% on the barbell. As the load is released at the bottom of the eccentric phase, an individual should raise the remaining 60% concentrically for 2 reps. The optimal amount of lifts for the 80% zone is 15 lifts.

What should be done when the main exercise of the work out is finished?

When a core lift is completed, exercises for the hamstrings, low back, glutes, hips and abs should be performed, such as:

- Glute Ham Raise
- Inverse Curl
- Reverse Hyper
- Pull a weighted sled
- Walking belt squat machine
- High rep leg curls with ankle weights
- Leg raise hanging or laying
- Sit ups
- Side bends

What would a brief example of what this system look like?

The Westside system is based on two workouts per week: one for speed and acceleration and 72 hours later one for a maximal effort. The max effort workout necessitates high intensity and low volume. The explosive or speed strength workout incorporates high volume while the intensity remains low. Improving in all special strengths allows one to progress not only speed and agility, but also technique. Learn how to perform specific, general and directed strength and as a coach you must lay out programs for:

- Barbell exercises
- Kettlebells
- Dumbbells
- Ankle weights
- Weight vests
- Sandbags
- Partner training
- Body weight only training

Major workouts should last approximately 60 minutes. Less resistance workouts should last 20 to 30 minutes. Finally, always use some methods of restorations such as:

- Water
- Massage
- Chiropractic
- Stretching
- Rubberbands
- Pharmaceutics
- Dietary

For further information please see The Westside Barbell Book of Methods, *The Squat and Deadlift Manual*, and read the free articles given on http://www.westside-barbell.com

Concluding Remarks

Please remember that weight training can make one more powerful and one's jumping ability more explosive. However, these two components must interact with each other. Using principles of physics, this statement can be further explained.

In physics work is defined as the product of the net force and the displacement through which that force is exerted or W=Fd. Power is defined as work done divided by the time used to do the work or P=w/t. Therefore, work defined in terms of sport could be a 100meter sprint, jumping 10ft, or jumping onto a 60" box.

Thus, the more powerful an athlete, the easier it is to perform the respective sport related work.

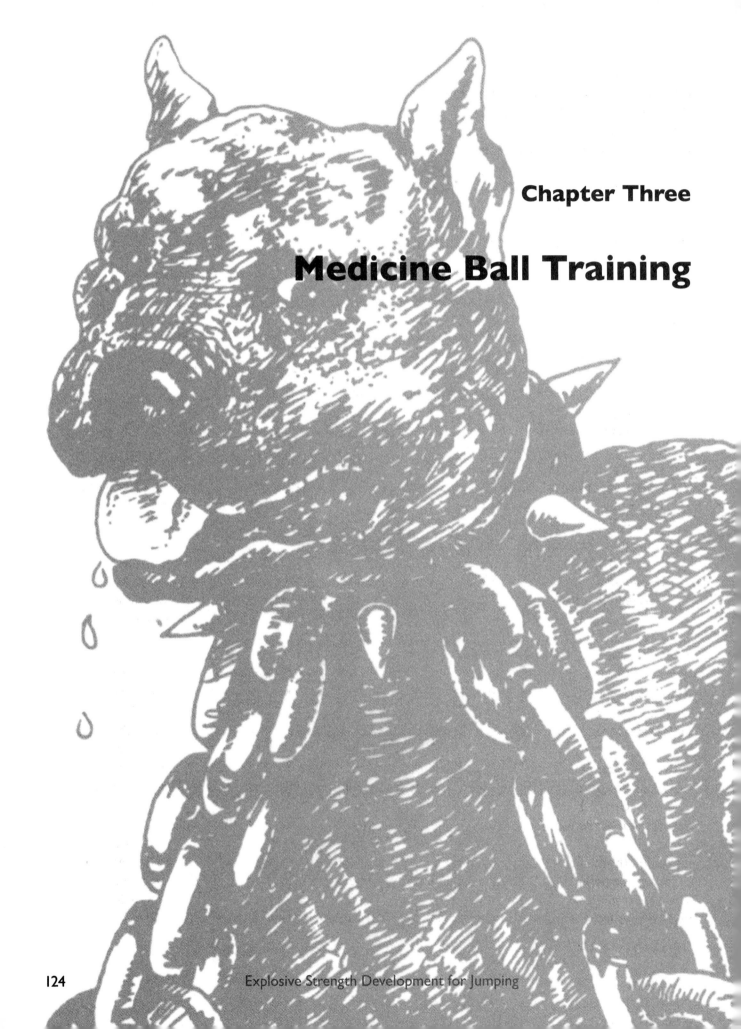

Chapter Three
Medicine Ball Training

Always have a plan to follow. Westside has many short plans consisting of one week or three weeks but no longer. By doing this, one's coach can monitor progress or lack of it before detraining or incorrect training resulting in poor performance.

Using upper body medicine ball work in an individual's reaction training can improve the ability to throw an object farther or to catch a ball and release it more explosively through the myostatic stretch reflex.

Tests

Implementing tests is imperative; therefore, most medicine ball exercises are performed in a catch and throw test.

- Standing throw forward
- Kneeling throw forward
- Standing throw overhead behind
- Kneeling throw overhead behind
- All above done with both arms or right or left arm only.
- Throw from a chest
- Overhead throw
- Side throw left and right
- Between legs to front
- Between legs to rear
- While laying in the sit up position

All tests can be made with a medicine ball or kettle bells of varying weights. Medicine ball throws are just another drill that falls under plyometrics, any exercise that explosively produces a stretch reflex.

While one can be very strong, he may lack explosive power due to a low rate of reversal strength. Upper body medicine ball work can overcome this dilemma.

Other methods include punching a boxing bag or a ball suspended by a rope or chain. The lower extremities can benefit from exercises with throws from the legs. See illustrations.

"Always have a plan to follow"

The medicine ball is vital in training all types of athletes. Every sport can justify its use, and there may be times when a medicine ball workout could be substituted for barbell training.

Medicine ball usage can help increase the ability to jump, to throw, or to increase one's speed and strength training while improving reaction times. In turn, medicine ball work is safe for the training of children as young as 10. This age should be duly noted as it the age when reactive strength, speed, quickness, agility, mobility can be greatly improved. Children should be supervised by a sports expert.

Extensive workouts can last 45 minutes or could be as short as 20 minutes with little rest between working sets. Changing workouts often is recommended to avoid boredom and accommodation.

Explosive Strength Development for JUMPING

General medicine ball work can increase the body's ability to rotate for throwing a ball, hitting a ball, or facing an opponent in combat sports.

Medicine ball work can build the upper body, lower body, and generally all muscles of the body. There are countless workouts and application with medicine balls.

They can increase general strength and conditioning. Reaction time can be increased by catching and immediately throwing medicine balls. Remember the larger or heavier the ball, the slower the amortization phase.

The amortization phase is the time from a jump landing to take off, or the time between the catch of an object and its release. The slower the eccentric phase, the longer the amortization phase can be.

The weight of the medicine ball should be determined by an individual's strength, age, and sport of concentration.

"The amortization phase is the time from a jump landing to take off"

Partner MB Over/Under Pass
Standing back to back with partner, bend down to pass medicine ball between legs; return to standing position; bring arms overhead to receive medicine ball.

Explosive Strength Development for Jumping

Partner MB Trunk Rotation
Standing back to back with partner, hold medicine ball in front of body; twist to the left, passing ball to partner;
return to center; twist to right, receiving ball from partner; return to starting position.

Med Ball Side Bridge
Execution; Start with a locked out arm and hand on a medicine ball. Then, ensure the upper and lower bodies form a straight line. Once this position is achieved, keeping the legs straight, take the top leg and place it several inches in front of the other, forming a "scissor" look with the legs.

Muscles used; Rectus abdominis, Obliquus abdominis internus, Obliquus abdominis externus, Spinal erectors, Deltoids, Teres major/minor, and Abductors.

Straight Arm Standing Med Ball Rotation
Execution; Start by standing with feet slightly outside shoulder width holding a med ball with arms locked. Keeping the feet flat, arms locked and the med ball close to the body, rotate in one direction until the med ball is behind the gluteus. Then, rotate in the opposite direction bringing the med ball across the lower abdomen. As it crosses the front of the body, begin to raise the ball as the torso rotation continues until the ball is shoulder width. Additionally, as the med ball is crossing the front of the body, the torso and hips turn in the direction of the rotation, allowing the opposite foot to plantar flex into the ground.

Muscles used; Deltoids, Rectus abdominis, Obliquus abdominis internus, Obliquus abdominis externus, Calfs, Trapezius.

V-Up Med Ball Handoff
Execution; Start by assuming the "V-Up" position with a med ball in one hand. Once there, hold the position while the med ball is handed off back and forth beneath the thighs.

Muscles used; Rectus abdominis, Obliquus abdominis internus, Obliquus abdominis externus, Hip flexors, Deltoids

Med Ball Overhead Reverse Crunch
Execution; Start by lying on your back with palms flat against the ground, legs straight and a med ball positioned between medial portion of the feet. Raise the legs continuously until the low back comes off the ground and the med ball gently touches the ground above the head.

Muscles used; Rectus abdominis, Hip flexors, Adductors, Spinal erectors.

Straight Leg Med Ball Handoff & Reach
Execution; Start by sitting on the ground, med ball in hand, torso upright, and legs straight. Then lift one leg, pass the med ball underneath and immediately go into a V-Up position while reaching the med ball up directly overhead until the arms are locked.

Muscles used; Rectus abdominis, Obliquus abdominis internus, Obliquus abdominis externus, Hip flexors, Deltoids.

Bounding Med Ball Toss
Execution; Start by standing with feet shoulder width, a med ball close to the chest and elbows loosely tucked to the side. In an explosive manner, drive and push off the back foot while driving the lead leg's knee and toe up. Finally, forcefully extending the arms, creating a projectile out of the med ball.

Muscles used; Gluteus, Hamstrings, Quadriceps, Calfs, Pectoralis major/minor, Anterior deltoid, Triceps.

Med Ball Squat Thrust

Execution; Start by standing with feet shoulder width and a med ball close to the chest and elbows loosely tucked to the side. Keeping the feet flat, squat down, the explosively reverse direction while plantar flexing the feet and forcefully extending the arms, creating a projectile out of the med ball.

Muscles used; Gluteus, Hamstrings, Quadriceps, Calfs, Pectoralis major/minor, Anterior deltoid, Triceps.

Explosive Strength Development for Jumping

Med Ball Swing & Release
Execution; Start by setting up in a wide squat position with the knees pushed out and med ball in hand. Then, keeping the back flat, reach the med ball as far back between the legs as possible. Finally, explosively drive up out of the squat position while swinging the med ball forward and releasing it at shoulder level.

Muscles used; Gluteus, Hamstrings, Quadriceps, Spinal erectors, Deltoids, Trapezius

Overhead Med Ball Toss & Jump
Execution; Start by standing with med ball held overhead by straight arms, and back slightly arched. In one explosive movement, contract the abdominals, plantar flex the feet to jump and release the med ball.

Muscles used; Rectus abdominis, Teres major/minor, Calfs.

Explosive Strength Development for Jumping

Med Ball Overhead Toss
Execution; Start by standing with feet slightly outside shoulder width, with med ball held in both hands. Then, keeping the shins perpendicular to the ground and head up, push the hips back and lower the torso while keeping the back flat. This motion will allow the med ball to pass between the legs, once this position has been achieved, explosively reverse direction. Push the hips forward and plantar flex the feet as the med ball is released directly above the head.

Muscles used; Spinal Erectors, Hamstrings, Gluteus, Calfs, Deltoids, Trapezius.

Med Ball Press Butt Kick
Execution; Start by squatting with feet at shoulder width and a med ball against the chest with elbows slightly tucked. Then, in one explosive movement, jump vertically while simultaneously touching the heels to the gluteus and pressing the med ball forward creating a rojectile.

Muscles used; Gluteus, Quadriceps, Calfs, Triceps, Pectoralis major/minor.

Med Ball Feet Scoop Toss
Execution; Start by standing with a med ball tightly secured between the feet. Then in one explosive movement, perform a half squat quickly reversing direction, once the legs are almost straight, fire at the hip flexors to drive the legs up, creating a projectile out of the ball.

Muscles used; Hip flexors, Quadriceps, Gluteus.

Med Ball Butt Kick

Execution; Start by standing with a med ball tightly secured between the feet.

Then drop into a quarter squat, explosively reversing direction. Flex the legs, keeping the toes pointed toward the shins, to bring the med ball to the gluteus.

Muscles used; Hamstrings, Quadriceps, Gluteus.

Explosive Strength Development for Jumping

Kneeling Med Ball Controlled Descent

Execution; Start by kneeling with knees at shoulder width, feet plantar flexed, and a med ball against the chest with elbows slightly tucked in. Then, extend the arms so as they are at a 45° angle. Next, in a controlled manner, press the hips forward keeping the core tight. Finally, when the med ball is about to create an uncontrollable descent, drop it and continue to control the descent as long as possible.

Muscles used; Gluteus, Deltoids, Trapezius, Rectus abdominis, Obliquus abdominis internus, Obliquus abdominis externus.

Kneeling Abdominal Med Ball Toss
Execution; Start by kneeling with knees shoulder width, hips pressed forward, feet plantar flexed, and arms fully extended overhead holding a med ball. Then in a controlled motion, continue to press the hips forward while arching the back and reaching the med ball with extended arms behind the body. After a slight pause, explosively contract the abdomen, releasing the med ball creating a projectile.

Muscles used; Rectus abdominis, Obliquus abdominis internus, Obliquus abdominis externus, Teres major/minor, Hip flexors.

Explosive Strength Development for Jumping

Single Leg Kneeling Abdominal Med Ball Toss

Execution; Start by kneeling with one up, one on ground (with plantar flexed foot), but both at 90° angles. Press the hips forward and have arms fully extended overhead holding a med ball. Then, continue to press the hips forward while arching the back and reaching the med ball with extended arms behind the body. After a slight pause, explosively contract the abdomen, releasing the med ball creating a projectile.

Muscles used; Rectus abdominis, Obliquus abdominis internus, Obliquus abdominis externus, Teres major/minor, Hip flexors, Quadriceps.

Med Ball Plank
Execution; Start by assuming the same position as a pushup, the main difference being that both hands are on the top of a med ball. Once in this position, keep the arms fully extended and hips up, creating a straight line composed of the neck, spine, and lower limbs.

Muscles used; Rectus abdominis, Obliquus abdominis internus, Obliquus abdominis externus, Triceps, Trapezius.

Explosive Strength Development for Jumping

Full Extension Med Ball Superman
Execution; Ly atop a plyo box stomach down with arms fully extended holding a med ball, hips on the edge of the box, legs straight, and feet plantar flexed. Keeping the arms extended, bring the med ball underneath the box. Finally, explosively contract the upper back to create a projectile out of the med ball.

Muscles used; Deltoids, Trapezius, Spinal erectors, Gluteus Hamstrings, Calfs.

Chapter Four

General Physical Preparedness – G.P.P.

G.P.P.

Following the general rule of three, a pyramid is only as tall as its base. For young athletes, a sound and large base of training is a necessity for the development of fitness, flexibility, agility, balance, and mobility. G.P.P. and S.P.P. join together as a unit, sometimes finding them connected closely together. For young athletes, it provides a well-balanced platform to launch a high level sports career.

For an older well-established athlete, G.P.P. can ensure a healthy, injury free training cycle and career. The work done by pulling a weight sled can build a strong body, which is capable of sustaining more and more advanced workouts. While a skilled athlete must perform more specific methods toward improving in a particular sport, I found this only to be true in a small or non-existing G.P.P. background. Performing mainly S.P.P., sport barriers will slow or stop further progress. Continuing G.P.P. in many special exercises or drills within a long sports career is possible. Everything discussed in this book will be addressed as G.P.P., leading into contest jumps such as:

- Long Jump
- Triple Jump
- High Jump
- Pole Vault

General sports training should start at ten-years-old; whereby, a child must learn simple sports tasks like swimming, volleyball, handball, and basketball for hand and eye coordination as well as improving agility, flexibility, mobility, and dexterity. This provides a wide base of general sports preparedness. Along with being able to run short distances, jump rope, use a trampoline, and be taught simple gymnastics, a child should also be able to perform push-ups, sits-ups, throw a ball, as well as be able to catch a ball. Before deciding what sport to specialize, a young athlete needs to be in good health. Also, if a young athlete does not like to hit or get hit, then combat sports are not advised. If running does not interest the child, then track may not be his sport. Young athletes should be put through a battery of tests that improve their chances of succeeding in a particular sport.

"A large base of training is a necessity"

G.P.P. can be raised by pulling a weighted sled hooked to the waist, using a light load going forward, backward, and sideways. Additionally, without any undue pressure on the spine, the sled can condition and strengthen the upper body through exercises such as: curls, presses, upright rows, judo throws, etc. one at the same time. Furthermore, a qualified coach is needed to guide one's career, fulfilling an athlete's potential.

General Endurance

One must have a high level of general endurance. Therefore, endurance is essential to sustain training with heavy workloads or overcoming difficult task such as: running long distances, or being able to shorten the rest time between workout sets.

Start with general endurance such as pulling a weight sled or repeated jumps or throws; then, mix general with special endurance.

When discussing G.P.P., concern must be placed on maintaining flexibility in the muscles, joints, ligaments, and tendons. Scheduling a program for flexibility and some form of relaxation after a large volume of training even with moderate loads or low volume heavy loads to speed up recovery is critical.

Recovery

The athlete must constantly work on developing flexibility that enables him to perform his sport injury free. To maintain maximum speed and strength, one also has to maintain and sometimes improve flexibility. A lack of flexibility can cause career ending injuries.

Flexibility workouts must be separate from sports workouts. In no study has it been shown that stretching before a sporting event increases performance. Just as absolute strength and endurance training should not be done simultaneously, flexibility workouts should be performed in three or four short 20 minute to 30 minute sessions, instead of one long workout, and they should include early morning stretching using a partner if desired. This improves agility and coordination for events from gymnastics to weight lifting. All ages should stretch on a regular basis. There are many forms of stretching, ranging from static, isometric, and dynamic. Learning when and where to utilize a particular method of stretching is crucial in furthering a sports career.

"Endurance is essential to sustain training with heavy workloads"

Standing Front Raise w/ KB
In standing position, raise both arms to shoulder level; return arms to side of body; repeat

Seated Front Raise w/ KB
In long seated position, raise both arms to shoulder level; return to starting position

Kneeling Front Raise w/ KB
Kneeling upright, raise both arms to shoulder level; return to starting position

Alternating Front Raise: Standing
Standing with feet hip width apart, raise right arm to shoulder level and lower back to side; raise left arm to shoulder level, lowering back to side

Explosive Strength Development for Jumping

Alternating Front Raise: Kneeling
Kneeling upright, raise right arm to shoulder level and lower back to side; raise left arm to shoulder level, lowering back to side

Alternating Front Raise: Seated
In long seated position, raise right arm to shoulder level and lower back to side; raise left arm to shoulder level, lowering back to side

Alternating Overhead Raise: Standing
Standing with feet shoulder width apart, hold one KB suspended at shoulder level while raising the opposite arm overhead; lower the raised arm to shoulder level, then raise opposite arm

Alternating Overhead Raise: Kneeling
Kneeling upright, hold one KB suspended at shoulder level while raising the opposite arm overhead; lower the raised arm to shoulder level, then raise opposite arm

Alternating Overhead Raise: Seated
In long seated position, hold one KB suspended at shoulder level while raising the opposite arm overhead; lower the raised arm to shoulder level, then raise opposite arm

Lateral Raise: Standing
Standing with feet shoulder width apart, hold KB's at the side of the body with arms straight; keeping arms straight, bring both KB's to shoulder height, raising arms laterally

Lateral Raise: Kneeling
Kneeling upright, hold KB's at the side of the body with arms straight; keeping arms straight, bring both KB's to shoulder height, raising arms laterally

Lateral Raise: Seated
In long seated position, rest KB's on thighs; keeping arms straight, bring both KB's to shoulder height, raising arms laterally

Explosive Strength Development for Jumping

Overhead Front Raise: Standing

Stand with feet shoulder width apart, hold KB's at the side of the body with arms straight; move both arms straight in front of body to an overhead extension

Overhead Front Raise: Kneeling

Kneeling upright, hold KB's at the side of the body with arms straight; move both arms straight in front of body to an overhead extension

Overhead Front Raise: Seated
In long seated position, rest KB's at sides of the body; move both arms straight in front of body to an overhead extension

Overhead Lateral Raise: Seated
In long seated position and arms extended, rest KB's on floor at sides of body; bring both KB's overhead by laterally raising straight arms; separate arms to laterally lower KB's (palms up) to ground

Explosive Strength Development for Jumping

Overhead Lateral Raise: Kneeling

Kneeling upright, rest KB's at side of body; bring both KB's overhead by laterally raising straight arms; separate arms to laterally lower KB's (palms up) to starting position

Explosive Strength Development for Jumping

Overhead Lateral Raise: Standing

Standing with feet hip width apart, rest KB's at side of body; bring both KB's overhead by laterally raising straight arms; separate arms to laterally lower KB's(palms up) to starting position

Explosive Strength Development for Jumping

Overhead Torso Rotation

Standing with feet hip width apart, rest KB's at side of body; raising arms to bring the KB's overhead, twist upper body to the right; return to center twist upper body to left (do not move feet)

Torso Rotation
Stand with feet slightly wider than hip width and KB's racked on shoulders; twist upper body to the right; return to center twist upper body to left (do not move feet)

Explosive Strength Development for Jumping

Standing Windmill: Straight Leg
With a KB in each hand and straight legs, keep both arms extended at the elbow; bend down to bring the left arm to the left foot while right arm raises overhead @ 180*; return to center; bend down to bring the right arm to the right foot while left arm raises overhead

Pendulum Swing
Bend forward and rotate body to the right and left; simultaneously swing KB across body with straight arms

Standing Windmill: Bent Leg

With a KB in each hand and feet apart, keep a slight bend in both elbows and knees; in a controlled motion, bend down to bring the left arm to the left foot while right arm raises overhead; return to center; bend down to bring the right arm to the right foot while left arm raises overhead

Cross-Body Windmill
Bend forward and rotate body, crossing the left arm to the left leg while right arms raises overhead; swing both KB's down in front over toes, crossing the right arm to the left leg while left arms raises overhead

Explosive Strength Development for Jumping

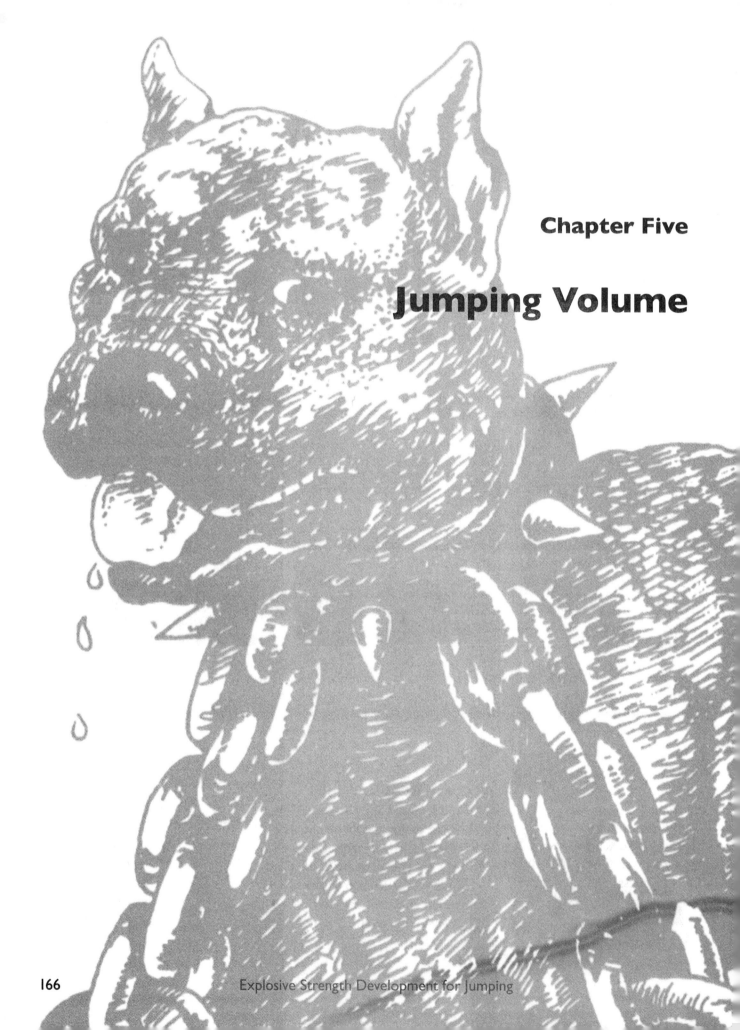

Chapter Five

Jumping Volume

Westside requires much less jumping than Yuri Verkhoshansky's program. This is so the speed strength barbell training sessions for pulling and squatting are more. Westside, like Verkoshansky, performs max effort workouts, but because an average of 80 squats are cycled a month in a 3-week pendulum wave plus 60 pulls a month the jumping volume is reduced.

- Depth Jumps 30" 4 x 10 jumps
- Depth Jumps 45" 3x 8
- Box Jumps Optimal 3x 20
- Bounding Optimal 4x 20
- Bar-in-hand Jumps 6x10
- Vertical Jump with Weight 8 x 3 jumps

Jumps are conducted with ankle weights, kettle bells, or weight vest. A combination of two or all three can be used. Forty jumps for intermediate and sixty jumps for national and international caliber jumpers can be implemented.

Westside Jump Recommendations

The main purpose of jumping is to improve explosive power to further the ability to jump higher or longer in special events in track and field. All sports that require great special strengths can benefit from implementing jumping.

Y.V. Verkhoshamsky, the father of plyometrics, discovered the phenomenon of the stretch reflex by watching triple jumpers perform. He was amazed by the powerful rebound on each preceding landing. Track and field and Olympic weightlifting have used the benefits of plyometrics for over four decades. Plyometrics can also elevate the standard for the power lifts. Westside has done numerous experiments with jumping. Our goal was to jump on the highest box possible without resistance other than air and gravity. Working with NFL players, NFL combine candidates, Olympic sprinters, and of course, world class powerlifters, we have developed a system to improve the maximum rate of force development using revolving jump drills that have made it possible to attain a 60-inch box jump.

Box Squat Box Jump

Sitting on a box about three inches above parallel, lifting the feet off the ground, and slamming them down again while jumping has produced the best technique for increasing a long jump or box jump for height. We know that as an athlete lowers himself onto the box, he represents potential energy. After contact with the box, he creates kinetic energy. The collision with the glutes and upper thighs isn't considered perfectly elastic, but rather inelastic. Add this to the feet being slammed on the floor and a large amount of kinetic energy is produced. This leads to the most productive method for increasing jumping ability. Pete Campion played as a lineman for five years for the NFL Raiders. A weekend visit to Westside earned him the longest long jump of his career. Pete had long jumped in high school and in the NFL, but in a span of 48 hours at Westside, he jumped further than ever before.

How?

By sitting on a 17-inch bench, rocking back and forth, picking up his feet, and then slamming them down before jumping forward. Another example is a 292 lb tight end from the Mac conference who ran a 5.1 second, 40 yard dash. I reduced his time to 4.9 seconds. After two months, he ran a 4.77 second 40 at his college professional tryout. The special jumping played a large role in his program. His school was an Olympic lifting school, and he had spent four years there wasting his time. Olympic lifting has very little to do with jumping. By the way, his long jump went from 8 feet, 9 inches to 9 feet, 8 inches. Everyone knows that we power lift. We don't run ball players, but rather jump, power lift, and power walk with weight sleds. I won't name his school or the strength coaches' names, but he still does the same old program.

Jumping with Ankle Weights

Jumps with ankle weights ranging from 5–40 lbs per leg are done on a variety of boxes. Ankle weight jumps are in sets of five jumps, and the emphasis is on strength. Thirty jumps are optimal with light weight. When using heavy ankle weights of 25–40 lbs, the jumps go down to 15 jumps. Single or double leg jumps should be altered.

Explosive Strength Development for Jumping

Dumbbell Box Jumps

John Stafford has jumped on to a 36-inch box with a pair of 70-lb dumbbells at a body weight of 290 lbs. A 290-lb tight end made a 36-inch box jump with a pair of 60-lb dumbbells. Again, we aim for 15–30 box jumps per workout. Use a combination of ankle weights and dumbbells.

Keep track of records of all types. This type of dynamic loading can be very taxing. Limit the weight jumps to no less than 72 hours between workouts. If you do depth jumps, start from 12–20 inches. Depending on whether or not you're an advanced 800-lb or more squatter, raise the box to 30–40 inches and land on approximately a 2-inch rubber mat. Drop straight down with your arms behind your body. After landing on the balls of your feet, lower on to the heels with your legs slightly bent. Swing your arms forward and jump upward explosively, landing in the same spot you jumped from. The aromatization phase will vary depending on how far you bend at the knees.

Weight vests can be used for jumping up on boxes on a regular basis. But you should only jump off of a box from a soft surface. Of course, jumping without arm swings can be done or jumping upward without an eccentric phase. Jump squats or step-ups are also a valuable tool. I prefer to do simple exercises for jumping. If jumping is that important—and it is—there should be special exercises to increase jumping. I am a fan and student of Starzynski and Sozanski. Check out the book.

Why do strength and jumping go hand in hand? They go hand in hand because the maximal velocity that can be displayed in a given movement depends heavily on the level of strength first and then coordination, flexibility, and technical skills. Strength first? Yes, this can be explained by junior weightlifters out jumping junior jumpers in the first three years. I am not a big fan of Olympic lifts for sports. The push jerk or press is the only element that contributes to jumping by the creation of an amortizing phase.

The support reaction in the phase is 233–245 percent of the bar weight, but I am a total believer in doing Olympic lifts from a seated knee position. While in high school, John Harper of Cincinnati could jump onto his feet from a sitting position on the ground with 170 lbs on his back. As a junior in college, he could jump about 195 feet. At this point, he could jump onto his feet with 265 lbs at a body weight of 265 lbs.

Our Sequence

1. Sit on the floor with your legs straight in front of you. Place a barbell on your upper thigh. Clean and press a bar over your head for several sets of 5–10 reps. Beginners should use several sets of 3–8 reps. Take rest breaks to ensure optimal recovery.

2. Set up on the knees. Sit back onto your glutes and jump onto your feet. After mastering this, place a barbell on your back and jump onto your feet. Later, jump up into a jump squat.

3. Sit on the knees, and sit back on the glutes with a barbell across the upper thighs. Jump up into a power clean.

4. Sit on your knees and then lower onto your glutes with a barbell across the upper thighs. Do a power snatch.

5. Sit on the knees, lower onto your glutes with a barbell across your thighs, and do a split snatch. Alternate for each leg.

It is best to do repetitions with the above exercises. Multiple jumps can be a common means of increasing jumping ability in all sports. These multi-jumps will increase jumping endurance, jumping ability, and sport specific strength (Mroczynski and Starzski, 1994).

I suggest jump roping first for timing, rhythm, and endurance. Master the kneeling jumps without weight first. These jumps are primarily for squatting and pulling power as well as increasing vertical jumping and box jumping ability. For long jumping, jump from the kneeling position without weight at first onto a low box. Our top jumpers can land on a 14-inch box from the knees. These jumps build a maximal rate of force development.

Seated Military Press
In long seated position, press weighted barbell from upper chest to locked arms

Kneeling Squat Jump
Kneel upright with barbell on back; dip slightly to load glutes; jump into squat position

Kneeling Squat Clean
Kneel down on a mat with the hips relaxed and barbell resting on lap; clean barbell into squat position while receiving with hips below knees; complete movement by standing up

Explosive Strength Development for Jumping

Kneeling Clean
Kneel down on a mat with the hips relaxed and barbell resting on lap; clean barbell into rack position

Kneeling Split Clean
Kneeling on a mat, keep hips relaxed with barbell resting on lap; explosively clean barbell to rack position while bringing one foot forward, resting on opposite knee

Explosive Strength Development for Jumping

Kneeling Squat Snatch
Kneeling on a mat, keep hips relaxed with barbell resting on lap; in one swift movement, jump to bring both feet to the ground as the barbell is received overhead, with hips below the knee; complete movement in standing position, arms locked overhead

Power Shrug
Begin with barbell just above knees; keeping arms straight, jump upright while explosively pulling bar off ground with upper back; return to starting position

Explosive Strength Development for Jumping

Half Squat Jump
Standing with barbell racked on shoulders, dip into a partial front squat; launch into an upward jump, keeping barbell racked; finish in starting position

Weighted Bounding
With barbell on shoulders, push off with the right foot, bringing the left leg forward (knee bent); hold this extended stride for a brief time before landing on the left foot; left leg then drives through to a forward bent position, and left leg extends back as right leg reaches in front; land on right foot

Explosive Strength Development for Jumping

Kneeling Good Morning
Kneel on a mat with body upright; reach hips back toward heels, flexing at the hips to lower upper body toward mat; return to start

Split Jumps
With barbell on back, place one foot forward into a lunge position; dip down, then push off balls of the feet to jump off ground; switch legs while in air, landing with opposite foot in front

Explosive Strength Development for Jumping

Weighted Squat Jumps
Begin in squat position with a loaded barbell resting on shoulders; explosively push off the floor against the weight, jumping upward; return to ground in squat position

Explosive Strength Development for Jumping

Weighted Step Ups (front)

With a barbell on your back, step onto a box in the following pattern:
  L-up > R-up
  L-down > R-down
  R-up > L-up
  L-down >w R-down

Explosive Strength Development for Jumping

Weighted Lateral Step Ups

With a barbell on your back, step laterally onto a box in the following pattern:

    L-up > R-up (to box)
    L-down > R-down (to ground, finishing on the opposite side of box)
    R-up > L-up (to box)
    R-down > L-down (to ground, finishing on the opposite side of box)

Deficit Squat Jump w/ KB

Place feet in squat position with each foot on a box of equal height; use the weight of a kettle bell to keep arms hanging straight in front to f body; jump upright so feet leave box; land in starting position

Explosive Strength Development for Jumping

Deficit Squat Jump w/Swinging KB
Place each foot on a box of equal height; jump vertically, swinging KB to eye level; land in deficit squat

Elevated Split Jumps
Use two boxes of equal height begin in a lunge position with the rear knee at the same level as the toe; jump high enough to transfer the lead leg to the rear, landing back into the lunge

Elevated Split Jumps: Decline

Use two boxes, with the front being slightly shorter than the rear; in a lunge position with the rear knee lower than the toe; jump high enough to transfer the lead leg to the rear, landing back into the lunge

Elevated Split Jumps: Incline

Use two boxes, with the front being slightly higher than the rear; in a lunge position with the rear knee higher than the toe; jump high enough to transfer the lead leg to the rear, landing back into the lunge

Explosive Strength Development for Jumping

Explosive Strength Development for Jumping

Lateral Step Up into Jump
Place left foot on box with right foot on ground; laterally step up to the box with right leg, transitioning into a vertical hop; return left foot to box and right foot to ground; step over (R-up L-up R-down); repeat jump with opposite leg

Explosive Strength Development for Jumping

Depth Jumps: High to Low

With feet hip width apart, stand on a large box with weight shifted into the heels; step down to the ground; landing on the balls of your feet, immediately rebound into a tuck jump; land on the next box slightly lower than the first

Depth Jumps: Low to high
With feet hip width apart, stand on a low box with weight shifted into the heels; step down to the ground; landing on the balls of your feet, immediately rebound into a tuck jump; land on the next box slightly higher than the first.

Explosive Strength Development for Jumping

Depth Jumps: Even

With feet hip width apart, stand on a box with weight shifted into the heels; step down to the ground; landing on the balls of your feet, immediately rebound up to the next box (same height as first)

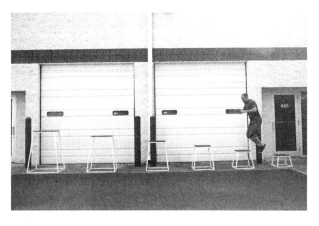

Multiple Depth Jumps
(Low to High; High to Low)

Set up several boxes, each increasing in height; standing on the lowest box, perform a depth jump (drop down to the ground, propel body forward and up) onto the next box; repeat until highest box has been reached; turn around and continue depth jumps, dropping from high box up to one of decreasing height

Explosive Strength Development for Jumping 195

Explosive Strength Development for Jumping

Explosive Strength Development for Jumping

198 Explosive Strength Development for Jumping

Explosive Strength Development for Jumping

Depth Jump into Broad Jump
Perform two depth jumps- one to a box of decreased height, then down to ground ; crouching down, swing arms and use momentum to leap forward onto mat

Explosive Strength Development for Jumping

Single Leg Depth Jump: High to Low (left leg)
Standing on a box; step down to the ground, with right foot suspended in air; landing on the ball of your left foot, immediately rebound up to a box of decreased height; land with right foot still suspended

Single Leg Depth Jump: High to Low (right leg)
Standing on a box; step down to the ground, with left foot suspended in air; landing on the ball of your right foot, immediately rebound up to a box of decreased height; land with left foot still suspended

Explosive Strength Development for Jumping

Single Leg Depth Jump: Low to High (left leg)
Standing on a box; step down to the ground, with right foot suspended in air; landing on the ball of your left foot, immediately rebound up to a box of increased height; land with right foot still suspended

Single Leg Depth Jump: Low to High (right leg)
Standing on a box; step down to the ground, with left foot suspended in air; landing on the ball of your right foot, immediately rebound up to a box of increased height; land with left foot still suspended

Explosive Strength Development for Jumping

Standard Box Jump: Seated Start
Begin seated on a box that allows your thighs to be parallel to the ground; rock back to lift feet off the ground, swinging arms to create momentum; shift body forward as feet plant down; spring forward off box; vertical jump up to a box of increased height; land in full squat position; stand

Double Box Jump into Broad Jump Combo: Seated Start

Perform standard box jump with seated start, onto a box of increased height; on landing, go directly into another box jump onto a box of equal height; drop down to ground using depth jump technique; crouching down, swing arms and use momentum to leap forward onto mat

Explosive Strength Development for Jumping

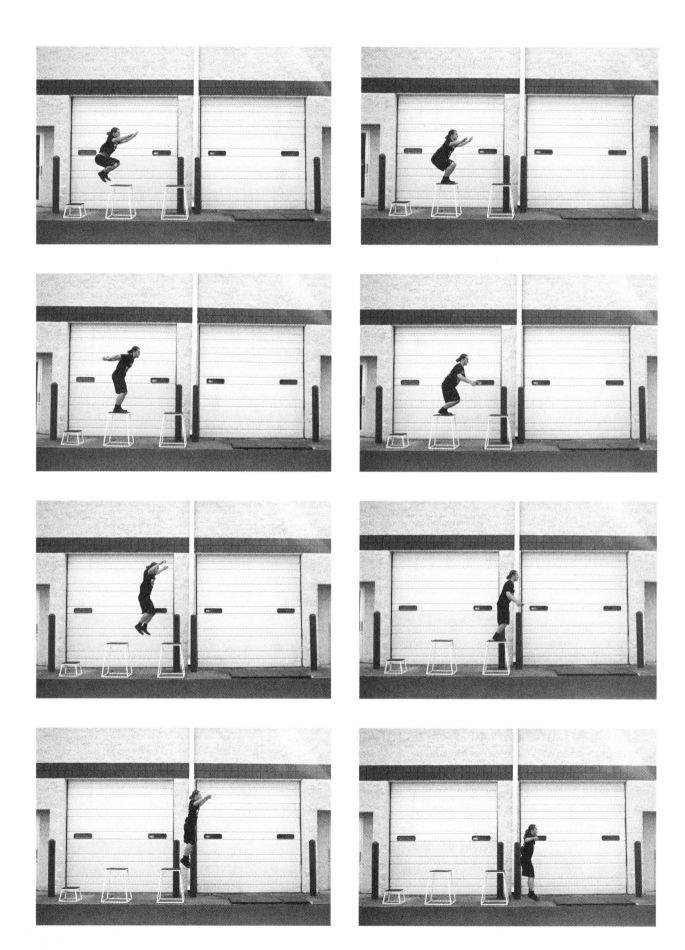

Explosive Strength Development for Jumping

Box Jump into Triple Jump Combo
Perform standard box jump with seated start, onto a box of increased height; drop down to ground using depth jump technique; immediately spring forward out of landing with hips completely extended; complete broad jump, landing on mat

Explosive Strength Development for Jumping

212 Explosive Strength Development for Jumping

Depth Jump into Triple Jump Combo

Perform a standard depth jump to the ground from a small box; using momentum, immediately perform a broad jump; jump from a crouching position onto a box of increased height; leap down and outward onto mat, landing in a squat

Explosive Strength Development for Jumping

Explosive Strength Development for Jumping

Depth Jump Rebound onto Foam Block
Perform a depth jump from a high box to ground; immediately rebound off balls of feet; jump forward and up, extending legs in front of body; land in long seated position upon foam blocks

Explosive Strength Development for Jumping

Depth Jump Rebound onto Foam Block (with KB's)

Perform a depth jump from a high box to ground; from standing take-off position, jump onto elevated foam blocks, keeping kettle bells in front of body; land with entire body extended and kettle bells at side

Kneeling Broad Jump

Start in kneeling position with hips relaxing on heels; swing arms behind body to gain momentum; as arms swing to front, quickly jump to crouching position, holding the squat at finish

Explosive Strength Development for Jumping

Jumping Heel Kicks
In standing position, prepare for take-off with a quick half squat down and up; jump upward, bending at the knee to bring heels to hips; return down to half squat at landing

Multi-jumps Over Obstacles (Standing Take-Off)

From a standing two-leg take off, perform a series of jumps over each obstacle, while pulling the knees into the chest; jump series can be done using 5-20 obstacles of varying or equal height

Explosive Strength Development for Jumping

220　Explosive Strength Development for Jumping

Explosive Strength Development for Jumping

Single Leg Multi-jumps Over Obstacles (right)
From a standing single-leg take off, perform a series of jumps over each obstacle, while keeping left leg suspended; jump series can be done using 5-20 obstacles of varying or equal height

Explosive Strength Development for Jumping

Single Leg Multi-jumps Over Obstacles (left)

From a standing single-leg take off, perform a series of jumps over each obstacle, while keeping right leg suspended; jump series can be done using 5-20 obstacles of varying or equal height

Explosive Strength Development for Jumping

Explosive Strength Development for Jumping

Upright Multi-jumps Over Obstacles (with pre-run)

From a running two-leg take off, perform a series of jumps over each obstacle; jump series can be done using 5-20 obstacles of varying or equal height

Explosive Strength Development for Jumping

232   Explosive Strength Development for Jumping

High Knee March over Hurdles
Keeping one leg straight, raise opposite knee high, keeping toes up; stepping over obstacle, place raised foot down, and flex opposite hip to bring other knee high; alternate arms throughout movement

Explosive Strength Development for Jumping

Chapter Six
Flexibility plus Agility

One must improve flexibility and agility at a high level and maintain that level throughout a sports career. There are several exercises that can contribute to movement coordination, flexibility, and agility. Basic gymnastic movements are a simplistic approach to accomplishing these goals. It is essential for the young athlete to learn, at the very least, simple gymnastic movements as not to limit his or her full potential in later years.

Many simple motor tasks cannot be learned even for athletes in their late teens. When doing tumbling and gymnastics, one must control rest intervals, remembering not to be too short in these movements because coordination can cause great fatigue. The word "flexibility" is always attached to stretching, but when and how long should one stretch? It is advised to stretch in the morning before eating if participating in activities that requires great flexibility. Remember to stretch muscles, joints, ligaments, and tendons.

Stretching using weights has been found to be of great value. If one can only squat to a 15-inch box, add weight with a wide stance. By doing several reps, the athlete can slowly achieve a greater depth. By simply taking a 1-inch mat off the box at a time, the athlete will be able to go lower and lower until reaching his desired depth. The upper body can reach to same results by using a cambered bench bar. Start with a 2 ½-inch cambered bar, after touching chest with a preset weight (ex. 135 lbs) move on to a 3 ½-cambered bar and later to a 5-inch cambered bar. This is a very basic, systematic approach.

"Many simple motor tasks cannot be learned even for athletes in their late teens"

Explosive Strength Development for Jumping

Everyone should stretch, from the very young to the very old.

Learn the many methods of stretching

Isometric stretching is the best method for dynamic, full range of motion of the joints. Static Active is where one learns how to relax stretched muscles by raising strength in the opposing muscles. Some refer to this as power strength. I highly suggest the purchase of Stretching Scientifically fourth edition 2003 by Thomas Kurz, Stadion Publishing Company, Inc. The aim is to raise mobility in the joints, achieve relaxation of the muscles and increase elasticity of the ligaments and tendons. This helps increase the ability to perform what is needed for sprinting and jumping, that being: RELAXED, EXPLOSIVE, and POWER.

Concluding Remarks

As one becomes more physically fit, two things happen: 1) a gain in fitness, 2) fatigue. This meaning that when one good occurs, one bad occurs too. The good, a gain in fitness from one workout is moderate and long lasting while the fatigue effect can be great, but not long lasting. The fatigue portion can lead to injury if one has a low level of flexibility.

Reverse Band Stretch

Muscles Used: Teres major/ minor, Pectorals major/minor, Deltoids, Trapezius, rhomboideus, Latissimus Dorsi

Picture A
Start with your hands behind your head while grasping the band, slowly lower until you feel on your shoulders, chest and upper back

Picture B
When the desire stretch is reached hold the position and inhale

Picture C
Begin to slowly exhale and lean forward while maintaining the stretch, repeat

Upper Body Stretching

Muscles Used: Triceps, anconeus, Deltoids, Pectorals Major/Minor, Latissimus Dorsi, Teres Major,

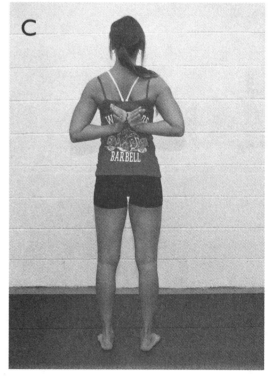

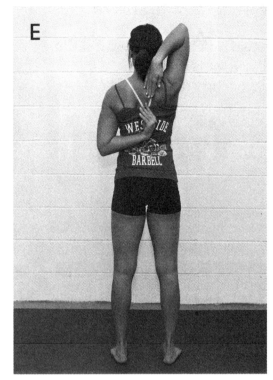

Picture A
Suprasspinatus.
Start with Interlapp of hands towards posterior. Keep full extension of arms then slowly raise up hands while maintaining full extension until desired stretch is reached.

Picture B
Start with interlocking fingers towards the posterior. Keep elbows flared out then slowly raise up interlocked hands while flaring elbows until desired stretch is reached.

Picture C
Start with elbows flared out posteriorly while back of the hands are placed together. Slowly raise hands up while flaring elbows until desired stretch is reached.

Picture D
Start with elbows flared out posteriorly while palms of the hands are placed together. Slowly raise hands up while flaring elbows until desired stretch is reached.

Explosive Strength Development for Jumping

Quadriceps Strech

Picture A
Start by standing vertically and grabbing the top of your toes. Slowly pull on your foot towards the gluteus.

Picture B
Keeping back straight touch ground with opposite hand until desired stretch is reached .

Standing Lower Body Stretch

Muscles used: Quadriceps, Gluteals, hamstrings, Adductors, Psoas, Piriformis Start with knee flexed and extend your non lead leg back until your feel desired stretch on calf. Progress by slowly lowering the torso to floor while keeping arms inside the lead leg. Finish by placing forearms with palms down on the floor.

Explosive Strength Development for Jumping

Side Low Body Stretch

Start with feet spaced apart. Extend lead leg out from the body keeping toes forward. Bend opposite leg to 90 degrees keeping toes forward and extended forward. When mastered progress to slowly lower groin towards the floor while lowering the trunk and extending arms outwards keeping palms faced down on the floor. When mastered progress to sink gluteals completely to the floor maintaining position while simultaneously re-adjusting hands to grab toes on lead leg.

Sitting Groin Stretch

Start by bending knees and place soles of feet together. Push down knees with elbows until desired stretch is attained. When mastered progress to relax neck and the lower and upper back neck, slowly exhale while gently pulling your torso forward and downwards placing hands out in front with palms facing down. When mastered place hands under knees, taking in a deep breath then slowly exhale while further pulling the torso downwards and pushing knees apart.

Straight Leg Hamstring Stretch
Start by sitting on the floor with both legs extended. Raise up both legs and grab beneath the knee joint. Take a deep breath in and exhale slowly while pulling legs towards the torso until desired stretch is reached. When mastered progress to single leg lift. Start with extending lead leg upward while keeping it straight, then grab toes with lead hand. Inhale deeply then slowly exhale and pull back until desired stretch is reached.

Standing Single leg Hamstring Stretch

Begin with a slightly staggered stance, keeping both legs straight, inhale deeply then calmly lower the torso down towards the ground while exhaling slowly aim, gently round the upper back and place hands palms down on the floor hold until desired stretch is reached. When mastered progress by picking up the toes on the stretched leg and gently move the arms back towards the body while keeping the palms on the floor hold until desired stretch is reached.

Standing Double Leg Hamstring Stretch

Start with both legs together and toes facing forward. Inhale deeply then calmly lower the torso down towards the ground while exhaling slowly aim, gently round the upper back while raising arms over the neck

Standing Groin-Hamstring
Execution; Start with feet wide apart holding ankle/low calf, then bend forward touching the floor with your head.
Muscles used; Adductors, Hamstrings

Abdomen Stretch "The Turtle"

Execution; Start by lying stomach down on the ground. Then flex the legs to get a hold of the ankles. Next, pull the ankles toward the back of the head while the torso is arched toward the ankles.

Muscles used; Rectus adominis, Obliquus abdominis internus, Obliquus abdominis externus Quadriceps, Psoas major/minor, Spinal erectors.

Abdomen Stretch "The Seal"

Execution; Start by laying stomach down on the ground. Then press into the ground with your hands, simultaneously raising the torso until the arms are locked at the elbow. Once locked, press the hips flexors into the ground while focusing also on arching the torso back.

Muscles used; Rectus abdominis, Obliquus abdominis internus, Obliquus abdominis externus Quadriceps, Psoas major/minor, Spinal erectors

Locked Leg Seated Side Bend

Execution; Start by sitting on the ground with legs locked split as far apart as possible with toes up. Then reach out to one side for the foot. Do not perform with a twisting motion or a lean forward.

Muscles used; Obliquus abdominis internus, Obliquus abdominis externus, Psoas major, Spinal erectors

Lying Knee Pull

Execution; Start by lying on your back, then holding the shin, pull on one leg toward the chest.
Muscles used; Gluteus

Seated Trunk Rotation

Execution; Start by sitting on the ground with toes up and legs locked. Spread legs approximately half way from their maximum stretched position. Then, keeping upright and chest up, rotate the torso in one direction. Whichever direction turned, the lead arm's hand strives to reach as far behind the body as possible while keeping upright. The following arm's hand should be in line with the hip being rotated toward.
Muscles used; Obliquus abdominis internus, Obliquus abdominis externus, Semispinalis, Transversospinalis.

Lying Banded Hamstring & Gluteus

Execution; Top (Hamstring); Start by placing the band around the arch of the foot, then lying back on the ground as both legs are locked and toes are up. Then, keeping leg locked, pull upon the band while rising the locked leg straight up as far as possible. Next, take the slack out of the band until it is taught, finally pulling this taught band until the desired stretch on the hamstring is achieved.

Bottom (Gluteus); Start by placing the band around the arch of the foot, then lying back on the ground as both legs are locked and toes are up. Then, keeping the leg locked, and both shoulder blades in contact with the ground, bring the leg across the body. Next, take the slack out of the band until it is taught, finally pulling this taught band until the desired stretch on the hamstring is achieved.

Muscles used; Top (Hamstring); Hamstrings Bottom (Gluteus); Gluteus

Seated Banded Chest & Shoulder

Execution; Top (Chest); Start by sitting on the ground holding a band greater than shoulder width. Then, keeping a slight bend in the elbow, rotate the band above and then behind the head. Keeping the band above the shoulders, allow the chest to relax as the band pulls the arms back.

Bottom (Shoulders); Start by sitting on the ground holding a band greater than shoulder width. Then, keeping a slight bend in the elbow, rotate the band above and then behind the head. Bring the band down to the mid-to-low back, allowing the shoulders to relax as the band pulls the arms back.

Muscles used;
Top (Chest); Pectoralis major/minor, Anterior deltoid
Bottom (Shoulder); Anterior deltoid, Rotator cuff

Low Back

Execution; Starting by lying on your back, bring the knees to the chest, then extend the legs, causing a roll backward. Plant hands in line with the ears while allowing the toes to touch the ground. Once in this position, relax the abdominals, thus allowing the low back to decompress.

Muscles used; Spinal erectors

Leg Swing

Execution; Start by posting against a wall or sturdy object. Then swing you leg forward (flexing the hip flexor) and back (flexing the gluteus). Maintain upright posture throughout movement.

Muscles used; Gluteus, Hip flexor

Cross Leg Swing

Execution; Start by posting against a wall or sturdy object. Then swing your leg bringing it away from the body, then across. Maintain upright posture throughout movment.
Muscles used; Abductors, Adductors, Piriformis

Explosive Strength Development for Jumping

Wall-Assisted Straight Leg

Execution; Start by standing against a wall with heels a few inches away. Then keeping legs straight, bend forward at the waist and with straight arms, place palms flat against the wall. Reach as far down as possible while still keeping the legs straight and palms flat against the wall. Once this position has been achieved, grab the part of the leg closest to each hand.

Muscles used; Hamstrings, Spinal erectors

Explosive Strength Development for Jumping

Elevated Hip Bridge

Execution; Start by lying on the ground and placing legs together atop a stable box so as the legs and thighs form a 90° angle. Then, place the hands palms down beside the head, thus creating a base. Next, contract the gluteus to lift the hips until the upper back comes off the ground and only the head and hands are in contact with the ground. Once in this position, focus on pushing the front of the hips as high as possible, creating not only a straight line, but a "bridge" or "arch" with the upper and lower bodies.

Muscles used; Gluteus, Hip flexors, Spinal erectors, Hamstrings, Triceps, Trapezius

Standing Hip Bridge

Execution; Start by standing approximately 4 feet from a wall. Then, keeping feet flat against the ground, reach back to the wall with a slight twist toward the arm reaching. Once one hand is placed on the wall, ensure the fingers are pointed down and palms are flat, then reach the opposite arm back and set that hand. Next straighten the torso, contract the gluteus, and press the front of the hips upward.

Muscles used; Gluteus, Hip flexors, Rectus abdominis, Triceps

Single Leg Leaning Hip & Hamstring

Execution; Start by slowly rising a straight leg to the rear. Keeping the back flat, keep the hands traveling along the shin while the leg continues to raise. Then place the hands with palms flat against the ground, while striving to keep the back leg straight and rising until both upper and lower bodies are in a straight line.

Muscles used; Gluteus, Hamstring, Hip flexor, Spinal Erectors

Kneeling Single Straight Leg Frontal Raise

Execution; Start by kneeling with the dorsal side of the foot flat on the ground, torso upright and shoulders back. Keeping one leg in the kneeling position, slowly extend the opposite leg until it is straight in front of the body, parallel to the floor, and plantar flexed. Once in this position, reach beside the body and behind the low back and join hands. Finally, while keeping the hands joined and arms locked, raise them toward the head.

Muscles used; Hip flexors, Quadriceps, Anterior deltoid, Pectoralis major/minor, Rotator cuff, Piriformis

Kneeling Single Straight Leg Lateral Raise
Execution; Start by kneeling with hips pressed forward and torso upright. Extend a leg laterally until it is straight, then plantar flex the foot so as the bottom is flush with the ground. Then raise the leg as high as possible while keeping it straight and foot plantar flexed.
Muscles used; Hip flexors, Abductors, Quadriceps

Lying Glute and Piriformis Stretch

Execution; Start by lying on your back. Then place the ankle of one leg across the opposite thigh. Next, reach and grab the opposite thigh and pull towards the chest. Muscles used; Gluteus, Piriformis

Seated Cross Leg Rotation

Execution; Start in a seated position with legs straight in front. Cross one leg across the body where the foot of this leg is on the opposite side of the opposing thigh and flat on the ground. Once it is in this position, the leg and thigh should be able to be "hugged". Then take the still straight leg and flex it toward the opposite glute. Finally, rotate the torso toward the glute of the crossed thigh.

Muscles used; Gluteus, Piriformis

Explosive Strength Development for Jumping

Partner Stretching

1/1 The Splits stretches the groin area along with the hamstrings, quads and hips.

1/4 Stand back to back with a partner and grasp hands above your head. This focuses on stretching the upper body and the back for the partner on top and for the partner on the bottom it does a deep hamstring and back stretch. Both partners will feel a stretch throughout the arms and hips as well.

2/4 As the partner on the bottom begins to lean forward, both partners will feel a deeper/longer stretch in the muscles.

3/4 The further the partner on the bottom leans forward the more both partners will feel a deeper/longer stretch throughout their muscles.

4/4 As both partners continue to hold this stretch, they will both benefit from a deeper stretch. The partner on the bottom will have a continuous stretch through their hamstrings and the partner on top will continue to feel the stretch throughout the back and abdomen region.

Explosive Strength Development for Jumping

1/3 With a partner, stand face to face with feet shoulder width apart and place your hands on one another's shoulders.

2/3 Bend forward and deepen the bend while lengthening the stretch. This will stretch out the arms, back, hamstrings, and the glute muscles.

3/3 Hold the position to continue to lengthen and stretch the muscles.

1/1 Stand back to back with a partner and reach your hands up, holding your partners hands. One person will rotate their body to the right as the other rotates their body to the left. This is great for stretching out the arms and upper back region.

1/2 Kneel down back to back with a partner; grasp your partner's hands overhead, this already beginning to stretch out the back and legs.

2/2 With your hands locked together proceed to move from kneeling to a standing position without letting go of your partner, this giving each person an overall body stretch throughout your arms, back, legs, and abs.

1/1 Stand face to face with a partner. Stretching the right arm forward, grasp hands and raise your right leg while holding your partner's right leg with your left hand. Make small jumps on your left leg, turning slowly to the right and then make small jumps back to the left.

1/1 Walk while holding your ankles and bending your knees as little as possible to get a good stretch through the hamstrings and glutes.

1/1 Squat down and walk while holding your ankles to get a better stretch through the quads along with the hamstrings and glutes.

1/1 If done properly, a handstand will lengthen, stretch and strengthen all the muscles throughout the body hitting mainly the upper body region.

1/3 Make a transition from a handstand to a bridge. Begin by holding the handstand.

2/3 Slowly come down and hold the bridge position to get a full body stretch through the arms, back, abs, and down through the legs.

3/3 This is an alternate view of a bridge stretch.

Explosive Strength Development for Jumping

1/5 Forward Roll -
Squat down with arms stretched out in front.

2/5 Place both hands on the ground, tuck your head and begin to let your body roll forward elongating the back muscles.

3/5 Continue to roll forward, rounding your back and keeping your feet together.

4/5 As you finish focus on keeping feet together and hands stretched out in front, while contracting you abs to assist in pulling yourself back to the squat position.

5/5 When finished you should be returned to your squatting position with feet together, arms stretched out in front.

Explosive Strength Development for Jumping

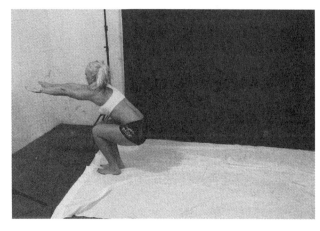

1/4 Backwards Roll - Squat down with both arms stretched out in front.

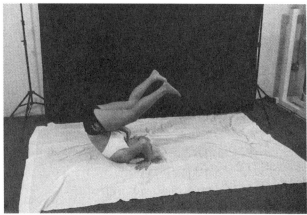

2/4 As you begin to roll backwards keep your legs together and hands placed on the floor. This will focus on a deep stretch through the upper back and shoulder region, along with a stretch through the hamstrings.

3/4 As you begin to land keep you abs tight and feet together to pull yourself back up and feel an allover stretch.

4/4 When finishing your roll, be sure to hold your squat position allowing a deep stretch in the quads and glutes.

1/4 Cartwheel – Start with your hands out in front and one foot in front of the other and begin to lean forward as you take a step.

2/4 Place your hands on the floor and kick your legs over while focusing on keeping your whole body tight.

3/4 As you land, bring one foot down at a time and contract your abs to have a solid landing.

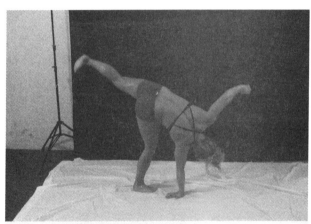

4/4 Return to standing and in an upright position like your beginning stance with hands in front and one foot in front of the other.

Explosive Strength Development for Jumping

1/5 Backwards roll into a handstand – Stand straight up with feet together, hands by your side.

2/5 While keeping your legs as straight as possible, bend at the waist stretching the hamstrings.

3/5 As you begin to roll backwards keep feet together, bring arms over your head and keeps abs tight to assist in the rolling process and get an overall stretch throughout your body.

4/5 Keep legs together and tight, keep abs tight and push straight up with your arms into a handstand.

5/5 With your body completely tight, keep your legs together and abs contracted and hold this position.

1/1 With a partner squat down across from one another while staying on up on your toes and begin to cockfight.

1/1 With both legs bent at the knees raise the buttocks and back off the floor supporting yourself with your arms.

2/2 While in this position begin to walk forward, one foot at a time allowing a long stretch through the legs, arms and shoulders.

1/1 The Wheelbarrow –
March on your hands while having your partner hold your legs at your ankle.

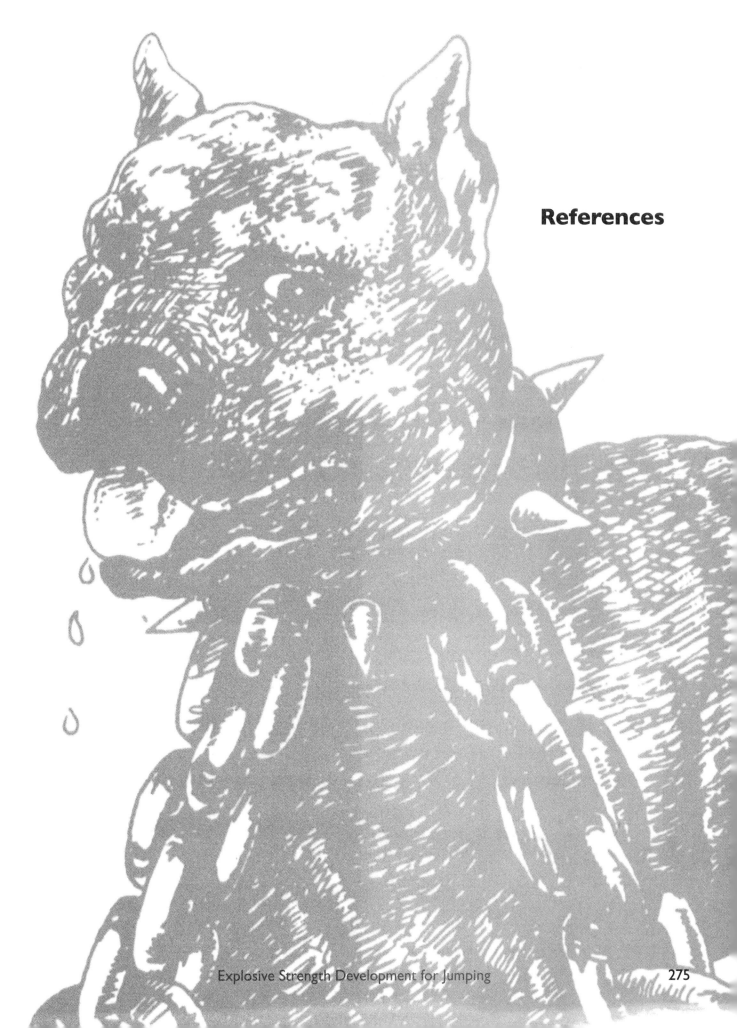

References

Allerheiligen. (1994). *Science of Sports Training*.

Bompa, T. (1995). *Power Training for Sports*.

Brunner, R. & Tabachnik, B. (1990). *Soviet Training and Recovery Method*. Sports Focus Publishing.

Charngia, A. (1992). *Weightlifting Technique and Training*.

Daniels, J. *Human Kinetics*. pp. 80-82.

Dvorkin, L. (1992). *Weightlifting and Age*. Michigan: Sportivny Press.

Fizkultura i Spovt. (1985).

Laputin, N. & Valentin, O. (1982). *Managing the Training of the Weightlifters*.

Medvedev. (1989). *A System of Multi-Year Training in Weightlifting*.

Medvedev, A.S. (1986). *A Program of Multi-Year Training in Weightlifting*.

Komi, P.V. (1992). *Strength and Power in Sport*.

Komi & Buskiak. (1972). Ergonomics. pp. 15, 417-434.

Kurz, T. (1990). *Science of Sports Training*. Island Pont, VT: Stadion.

Laputin, N.P. & Oleshko V.G. (1982). *Managing the Training of Weightlifters*.

Roman R.A. (1986). *The Training of the Weightlifter*.

Romanov, N., PhD. *The Pose Method of Running*.

Ross, B. (2005). *Underground Secrets to Faster Running*.

Sherrington, C. (1906). *The Integrative Action of the Nervous System: A Centenary Appreciation*.

Siff, M. (2003). *Supertraining*.

Siff, M. (2004). *Supertraining*.

Simmons, L. (2007). *Westside Barbell Book of Methods*.

Starzynski, T. (1995). *Power and Jumping Ability for all Sports*.

Suleymanoglu, N. & Turkileri, Y. (1997). *The Pocket Hercules*.

Tabalhnik, B. & Papanov, V. (1987). *Sprinters from the G.D.A. Leg Kaya Atletika.* Soviet Sports Review. 8:16-18.

Turkuleri, E. (2004). *Naim Suleimanoglu: The Pocket Hercules.*

Verkhoshansky, V.M. (1997). *Fundamentals of Special Strength Training in Sports.*

Verkhoshansky, Y.V. (1985). *Programming and Organization of Training.*

Weightlifting Yearbook. (1985). A. Charniga, Trans.

Weightlifting Yearbook. (1983). A. Charniga, Trans.

Weightlifting Yearbook. (1981). A. Charniga, Trans.

Weightlifting Yearbook. (1980). A. Charniga, Trans.

Westing. (1988). *European Journal of Applied Science.*

Yessis, M. (1987). *Secrets of Soviet Sports Fitness and Training.*

Zatsiorsky, V.M. (1995). *Science and Practice of Strength Training.* Champaign, IL: Human Kinetics.

Notes

Notes

The Westside Barbell Book of Methods

Over the many years Louie has been involved in powerlifting, he has gained a vast amount of knowledge on how to generate strength. It is this experience that has produced numerous national and world champions in different sports. Lou has helped many athletes in various sports, like World record holder 400m dash Harry "Butch" Reynolds. Also, Louie's methods of training have resulted in thirty-four 700 lb benchers, ten 800 lbs benchers and two athletes who have benched over 900 lbs. Westside Barbell also has twenty athletes who have deadlifted 800 lbs, twenty athletes who have squatted over 1000lbs, five athletes who have squatted over 1100 lbs, and two athletes who have squatted 1200 lbs or more. The numbers you read here are results from members of a small, private club.

Percent training method
Conjugate training method
Dynamic training method
Maximum effort method
Lifting techniques
Raising work capacity
Rehabilitation and restoration
Reactive and contrast methods

As a result of Louie's experience and knowledge, over 300 training articles have been published and 9 training DVDs produced. He is a strength consultant for the Cleveland Browns, Green Bay Packers, New England Patriots, Seattle Seahawks, and numerous other college football teams along with many athletes around the world.

This book is based on Louie's articles and offers a total Westside package. It leaves no stones unturned, and it is a perfect tool for lifters and coaches. This book will teach you to coach yourself.